WORKING
IN US WHAT
IS PLEASING
TO HIM

Paul Nordman

XULON PRESS

Xulon Press
2301 Lucien Way #415
Maitland, FL 32751
407.339.4217

www.xulonpress.com

Endorsements

Paul Nordman brings a fresh and thoughtful approach to helping us walk with God in *Working in Us What is Pleasing to Him*. I love how he extracts wisdom from a variety of biblical characters, everyday people whose examples challenge and help us lead transformed lives. Paul writes not just to inform the head or to simply inspire the heart but to encourage and challenge us to be transformed into the likeness of Christ. Paul's fresh insights from the Scriptures and personal stories will stimulate your heart and life to be more like Jesus—the goal of transformation.

—Bill Mowry
Author of *The Ways of the Alongsider*

Belief in Christ is the first step in our transformation into His image. But how does this happen, and what is my part? Why would God even bother with me? If this sounds familiar, read my friend Paul Nordman's book, *Working in Us What Is Pleasing to Him*. Throughout its pages, we see ourselves reflected in the lives of twelve unforgettable personalities of the Bible and their transformative encounters with God, for He still overcomes our brokenness and draws our hearts and minds to Himself. This book is encouragement in our weakness and a celebration of God's triumph in us. I recommend it to you.

—Mark A. Voltmann

Chairman, Educational Media Foundation (KLOVE and Air1 Radio)

Paul's latest book, *Working in Us What Is Pleasing to Him*, reminds us of God's amazing love and grace that surpass our natural understanding. Paul connects the experiences of twelve Biblical characters with our current-day reality to present a refreshing opportunity for honest self-reflection that points us to Jesus Christ. Paul's latest effort reminds us God continues faithfully today to transform the lives of His children! This is a special read that will leave you feeling renewed, eager to serve, to love as Jesus endlessly loves us and to live a life of divine purpose.

—Dr. Benjamin R. Buchanan

The Ohio State University Sport Industry Faculty and ABC/ FOX Broadcasting

Endorsements

Paul purposefully, passionately, and persuasively leads us into the deep recesses of God's transforming grace. In so doing he stimulates confidence in God and joyful cooperation with His work in us. Paul's use of relatable examples and analogies dramatically illustrates the truth of grace transforming us to be like Christ. If you want to joyfully run the race with grace, read this book!

—Rich Mendola
CEO, International Friendships, Inc.

Table of Contents

Table of Contents

A Helpful Introduction

S ipping coffee one morning in a bakery café, I could not help but overhear the Bible study leader at a nearby table. "We're saved by grace, but the rest is up to us," he declared to his listeners. There it was—I had heard this before and found it, again, to be frustrating. A bolder believer might have walked over and skillfully wheedled his way into their conversation, but there I sat just a few tables away, deflated in disappointment and content to rehearse the apostle Paul's rebuttals in silence. "Did you receive the Spirit by the works of the law, or by believing what you heard?" I echoed his argument in the inaudible tones of the mind, "After beginning by means of the Spirit, are you now trying to finish by means of the flesh?"[1] Oh, what burdens we needlessly accept for ourselves and carelessly place on each other.

As we look back on our life in Christ, isn't it true our growth in Him has come in the manner of changes only God could have brought about in us—some of which we realized at the

---

[1] Galatians 3:2–3

time, and even more of them crystalizing in the clarity of hindsight? Doesn't a great sense of confidence and joy come from evidence of His silent handiwork in our life, the fruit of which most often appears to our grateful surprise? If anything, part of the Spirit's transforming work in us is to dismantle the prideful notion we can undergo spiritual metamorphosis by our own effort, as if self-willed behavior modification were its equal.

God Has a Vision for Us

God has a vision for us. "What we will be has not yet been made known," writes John, but we do know this: "when Christ appears, we shall be like him."[2] We know, also, that what we will be is beyond our current ability to comprehend, for God's Word uses the term "glory" to describe it. The apostle Paul tells us that, as we contemplate Jesus' glory, we are being changed "into his image with ever-increasing glory, which comes from the Lord, who is the Spirit."[3] He writes elsewhere, "When Christ, who is your life, appears, then you also will appear with him in glory."[4] Our minds cannot take us there; we can read all we want and imagine as we will, but we cannot grasp what God has in store for us any more than we can fathom the dimensions of the love from which He changes us into the likeness of His Son.

---

[2] 1 John 3:2
[3] 2 Corinthians 3:18
[4] Colossians 3:4

God brings us to His vision state through a process called transformation. It transcends mere growth, though maturity is part of its process, to create a more radical change—a metamorphosis of our being. A caterpillar grows into a larger version of itself, for instance, but it takes metamorphosis for it to become a butterfly. Through such a transformation, then, God effects His plan for us—"to be conformed to the image of his Son."[5] This is His doing. How could it possibly be "up to us," as asserted in the coffee shop that morning? We can no more transform ourselves than we could save ourselves. Just as we step solely into Christ for salvation, so we also entrust ourselves entirely to His Spirit to transform us. It is He who changes us steadily to become like Jesus.

We Have an Active Role

Have you noticed yet the passive language of transformation? Paul says we are predestined *to be conformed* and we are *being transformed*, and he urges us *to be transformed.* Then is our spiritual journey mere slumber at the wheel of a self-driving car? Hardly. It is clearly the Spirit of God who changes us; our role, then, is to cooperate with Him as He does so. We offer ourselves to God for His purposes, and we resist the one who would tempt us to do otherwise. We empty ourselves of that which would distract or dissuade us, and we fill up on the

---

[5] Romans 8:29

Word of God and run in the presence of His Spirit. We submit our minds to Him who is truth and dispel every untrue thought and deception. We remember what we once were, and we trust in Him who made us who we now are. We say no to those who would restrain us again under caterpillar law—as though we could fly without wings if we just tried a little harder—and we float instead as new creatures on Spirit winds. We live in the obedience that comes from faith.

Just Like Us

Jiashang's academic advisor had recommended he improve his spoken English skills if he wanted to become "a more serious doctoral candidate." So I asked my international student friend if he wanted to meet with me weekly for coffee, tea, and conversation. He did, and at some point in our second one-on-one, he asked, "Do you think you could teach me some Bible stories?" I kept my best poker face and said, "Sure, we could do that," my heart leaping at the thought, "How would you like to go about it?" "I was thinking maybe we can learn about Jesus' disciples," he replied. It was an unconventional approach, which seemed refreshing and intriguing. Count me in! We began with the disciples about whom there is but mere mention—Thaddeus, Bartholomew, and Simon the Zealot, for instance—and made our way toward those more prolific in Biblical ink. By the time we visited Nathaniel, Philip, and Thomas, Jiashang had come to realize these were ordinary people. "They're just like us," he quietly observed, much to his surprise.

Yes, they are, and how liberating the thought. The men and women whose stories fill Scripture like busts in a hall of fame are fallen people; none of our forebears—save One—are there because they deserve to be; rather they live on in perpetual witness of the glory and grace of God's work in His people. Who better, then, to teach us about the promise and means of transformation than these whose life stories resemble our own? Naomi, for instance, traveled the road from bitterness and loss to the restoration of joy—her life has much to say to us— and Thomas finally straightened up from his slouching posture of doubt to stand tall in the confident stature of belief. If Zacchaeus exhibits evidence of immediate transformation upon welcoming the Savior into one's life, then Jacob bears witness also to its pausing, persevering pace.

Who better, then, to teach us about the promise and means of transformation than these whose life stories resemble our own?

Are you trying to become Christlike by your own natural wisdom and strength? Peter can show you the better way of the Spirit. And what do a Roman centurion and a Samaritan woman have in common? Both show us transformation does not stop at us but flows through us to bear fruit far beyond the borders of our imagination and long after we're gone from here.

Joseph's life alerts us that forgiveness is essential to healing and growth, while David's story shows us the value of others who speak good into our life. We'll visit a former demoniac, whose life testifies first to the unsurpassed authority of Christ over "the powers of this dark world,"[6] and also to the joy of kingdom usefulness as one set free from their grasp. In Paul, we see the irreplaceable role of suffering in transformation, and, finally, John teaches us what it means to be made complete in love. Twelve broken people "just like us"—through these we will see for ourselves the guts and glory of being changed into the likeness of Christ, of becoming "just like Him."

As we learn from each of the figures featured in this book, we will likely find ourselves identifying more with certain individuals than to others, as for better or worse, some more closely reflect our own temperaments, traits, and life experiences. Personally, I identify with Jacob and Thomas, for in them I see vividly both my natural inclinations and, thankfully, the working of God's refining grace in my life. For you, it may be Paul's legalism-shattering step into faith that speaks most clearly to your soul, or perhaps like Joseph you find the balm of forgiveness emancipates you from the pain of the past and heals you for the journey forth. The commonalities we share with these and others encourage us in hope, for in them we see God's vision for us and his faithfulness to bring us to

---

[6] Ephesians 6:12

glorious completeness, just as He has done in countless people "just like us."

Personal Reflection and Group Discussion

As with my first book, *Christ in Me*, I have written *Working in Us What Is Pleasing to Him* as a resource for personal reflection and growth, yet its structure conveniently lends itself to group discussion as well. For each of the twelve Biblical characters featured here, there is a brief introduction, followed by four short teaching-reflections. Should your small group choose to use this book for discussion and growth, I recommend you immerse yourself in one of its twelve sections each week. On day one, read through the introduction and all four reflections to develop an overall frame of reference, then on days two through five, dive deeper into each individual reflection. When you gather together, listen and learn how that week's study resonated among people in your group, and grow in your understanding and appreciation of each member. Celebrate the differences among all who unite and serve as one in the body of Christ.

Whether you use this book as a resource for your personal devotional time or as a means for group growth, take some time at the end of each reflection to consider these questions.

Can you relate through personal experience to this reflection? If so, how?

What peace, strength, comfort, or encouragement can you take from this teaching?

Reflect on at least one way today's reading helps you see more clearly the Spirit's work in transforming your life. How would you share this story of transformation with others?

In what specific way today can you respond to the Spirit's ongoing transformational work in you?

Finally, I encourage you, as you finish reading and meditating each day, to set this book aside and talk with God. He loves you.

> *Now may the God of peace, who through the blood*
> *of the eternal covenant brought back from the*
> *dead our Lord Jesus, that great Shepherd of the*
> *sheep, equip you with everything good for doing*
> *his will, and may he work in us what is pleasing*
> *to him, through Jesus Christ, to whom be glory*
> *for ever and ever. Amen. (Hebrews 13:20—21).*

o all of you who live in Christ by faith and engage this world in the power of the Spirit—you encouragers who strengthen through voice and presence, you helpers who prove faith through action, you teachers who skillfully open the Scriptures, you givers who eagerly open your wallets, you intercessors from the heart, you leaders unswerving from truth, you evangelists proclaiming good news, you administrators who organize chaos, all who hear the Spirit's voice and obey: God does awesome things through your submitted hearts, inspired words, and available hands. May you find courage, strength, peace, and joy in these pages.

Section One

Zacchaeus

S tanding tall among the more endearing stories in the Bible is the historical account of Zacchaeus. As Jesus of Nazareth passed through the city of Jericho, this determined and diminutive businessman, undaunted by public opinion, ran ahead and scaled a sycamore tree, hoping to peer over the gathering crowd and catch a glimpse of Him. We do not know what, if anything, he expected to gain by a peek at the traveling teacher—perhaps nothing more than curiosity quenched—but what he could not have anticipated was this: Jesus wanted to see him too. A tax collector, and worse, a *chief* tax collector, Zacchaeus had become wealthy by despicable means and was scorned by the people for his profession, but Jesus was coming to *his* house. From that visit, we can see what might have been for another rich man, the young ruler who, though careful to keep the commandments all his life, could not will himself to do what this repentant "sinner" gladly did from the heart—part with his possessions and give to the poor. One went away from Jesus sad; the other celebrated in His presence with joy.

Who knows what Jesus said to His grateful host in the comfort of his hospitality that day? Who knows why Zacchaeus responded to Jesus the way he did, welcoming Him not only into his home but into his life as well? Maybe he had served money long enough and devotedly enough to realize its penchant to tantalize but refusal to satisfy. Perhaps he saw in Jesus a richness from a kingdom where earthly currency does not spend. Whatever transpired in his home that pivotal day, Zacchaeus retired to bed a different man than the one who had awakened that morning, far less wealthy—perhaps no longer wealthy at all—but much more alive, for "salvation [had] come to his house."[7]

His story is an uplifting one, a legacy that began humbly enough with this simple desire: Zacchaeus wanted to see who Jesus was. What he found was salvation and the joy of a life transformed by grace. Zacchaeus became a new man emancipated from an old god—money—for in one encounter with Christ, this cheating taker became a cheerful giver. We learn this from him: though transformation into the likeness of Christ takes a lifetime, it begins at once. Watch and see.

---

[7] Luke 19:9

He Sought Us First

"**H**e wanted to see who Jesus was."[8] The chief tax collector may have been short in height, but he was big on desire—determined, a doer, we might say. So when Zacchaeus set out to see Jesus, not even the towering crowd would stand in his way. He found a suitable sycamore, climbed to an acceptable height, and waited—a curious man curiously perched in a tree. What happened next is something no one of any stature could have seen coming. "Zacchaeus," said Jesus, stopping now and looking up at the man, "come down immediately. I must stay at your house today."[9] The tax collector knew the scorn of religious people, but this man of God was different—engaging and unafraid to befriend a person cast off by others as "a sinner."[10] *And He had called him by name.*

With the exception of a couple of notable exchanges, we are not privy to any detailed conversation that ensued between the rich man and his house guest that day, but we do know this: he who had harshly seized from others amounts they did not owe now humbly received from God a gift he could not earn—salvation. This grace would change Zacchaeus immediately and forever. "Look, Lord!" he exclaimed, "Here and now I give half of my possessions to the poor, and if I have

---

[8] Luke 19:3
[9] Luke 19:5
[10] Luke 19:7

cheated anybody out of anything, I will pay back four times the amount."[11] Said Jesus in reply, "Today salvation has come to this house."[12] Indeed it had, spiritual birth already bearing spiritual fruit.

Luke opened this gospel narrative with Zacchaeus wanting to know who Jesus was, but the story began quite differently and long before then. It began in the heart of God, "For the Son of Man came to seek and to save the lost."[13] It is Jesus who seeks *us*, corporately as a people and personally as individuals. When He stirs in us, we look up and seek Him too—the sheep recognizing his Shepherd, the created reconciled with her Creator, neither content with separation but each finding joy in the other. Then being born of the Spirit, we begin to grow as He transforms us into the likeness of Him who knows us best, loves us most, and calls us by name.

I have gone astray like a lost sheep; seek your
servant, for I do not forget your commandments.
(Psalm 119:176 ESV)

Father, thank You for sending Jesus to seek and to save the lost. Thank You for sending Him to seek and to save me. Change me to be ever more like Him. Amen.

---

[11] Luke 19:8
[12] Luke 19:9
[13] Luke 19:10

What We'd Really Like To Be

An attorney once told me, "Do you know what I'd really like to be? A gym teacher." Chalk up one more for the "golden handcuffs," the allurements in life—income, status, or power, for instance—that entice us away from what we really want to do, be, or become. More sinister are the temptations that, perhaps one small step at a time, coax us away from what we know to be right and down a deceptive path to disillusionment and despair. We awake one day in a place that seems far away from God and see no way back to Him, but this too is a temptation—the temptation to doubt God's seeking love and His saving power. Perhaps this was Zacchaeus' path earlier in life, an incremental departure from the ways he knew to be good and right. Yet God knows our proclivity to stray, and in persistent love He draws us back to Himself, where we find a new and refreshing life of purpose. "God's Kingdom is near!" proclaimed Jesus as He traveled from town to town, "Turn from your sins and act on this glorious news!"[14] It remains today a refreshing invitation to change course.

Prominent among all we learn from Zacchaeus in ten short Biblical verses is this: the change to which God calls us is not an obligation to endure, but the opportunity we desire. Despite his wealth, and perhaps illumined by it, Zacchaeus found the greater and enduring treasure of life in God and the value of people made

---

[14] Mark 1:15 TLB

in His image. "Look, Lord!"[15] exclaimed the liberated tax collector, and with glowing excitement like that of a child, he overflowed in fulness of life, giving what he did not need to those who did not have and restoring to others what he had taken from them—their money, certainly, and perhaps their hope. His was not the *"have to"* duty of penance but the *"get to"* enthusiasm of

The change to which God calls us is not an obligation to endure, but the opportunity we desire.

release. Behind him lay the discarded handcuffs he once thought golden and before him "the unfathomable riches of Christ."[16] The taker had become a giver, and the giver had found joy.

Most of us do not need to be convinced of our wrong turns in life or the directions in which they have sent us; we are well acquainted with them and have lived to regret them. What we need to realize is that God calls us, saves us, and then leads us for a lifetime through the change our renewed hearts desire. We will become what we'd really like to be—like Him.

> *You make known to me the path of life; in your presence there is fullness of joy; at your right hand are pleasures forevermore. (Psalm 16:11 ESV)*

---

[15] Luke 19:8
[16] Ephesians 3:8 NASB

Zacchaeus

Father, it is a privilege to know Your love; it is a relief to know Your redemption; it is an honor to walk Your paths. Send Your Spirit to lead me in Your ways and use me for Your glory. In Christ I pray. Amen.

Just the Beginning

"You're walking into a mess," my mother-in-law said in a fair-warning tone. Peggy had gone to visit her for the weekend, and upon arriving, learned a pipe had succumbed to Michigan's winter temperatures, bursting and flooding the furnished garage apartment that stood a short distance from the house. Where does one start amid so much damage but at triage? So that is what Peggy did—assess the situation, begin at "first-things-first," and go from there.

Most of us would agree that when Jesus comes to us, He too walks into "a mess," a spiritual one. What we learn from the story of Zacchaeus, fortunately, is that God does not leave us that way; He begins at once to restore us from the inside out. For a chief tax collector turning from greed, first-things-first was generosity: "Here and now I give..."[17] There was no hesitancy at the Spirit's voice, no second-guessing, and no delay— just obedience. Next-things-next, then, was the promise of restoration, "I will pay back ..."[18] Zacchaeus was on his way, an exciting beginning to a lifetime of transformation, for greed was not his only sin, nor would all of his change be immediate.

We only come to know our heart as God reveals it. "My conscience is clear, but that does not make me innocent,"[19] Paul confessed of his natural inability to know the depth of his own

---

[17] Luke 19:8
[18] Luke 19:8
[19] 1 Corinthians 4:4

sin. "Search me, God, and know my heart; test me and know my anxious thoughts,"[20] implored David, for he himself could not fully understand either one. Yet these, our shortcomings, ultimately glorify God, for He does know the depth of our sin, and His love reaches deeper; God does know the breadth of our wrongs, yet His forgiveness reaches wider. God knows our "mess," and He transforms us in His time.

Occasionally we wonder if we have progressed at all in our relationship with God. In such times of discouragement, we do well to remember it was Jesus who "came to seek and to save the lost."[21] He is the initiating God, and He finishes what He starts, so with the confidence of Paul, we can live in the assurance that "he who began a good work in you will carry it on to completion until the day of Christ Jesus."[22] Salvation is just the beginning.

Father, thank You for sending Your Spirit to change me increasingly into the image of Your Son. When I am discouraged, may He remind me of the work He has already accomplished and assure me of His faithfulness to complete what He has already begun. Amen.

---

[20] Psalm 139:23

[21] Luke 19:10

[22] Philippians 1:6

Receiving Far More

W ho in his day would have predicted Zacchaeus to endure as one of the more endearing characters in the Biblical record? Sunday School children gleefully sing of this "wee little man," and his determination and enthusiasm warm hearts of every age. Beyond all the feel-good facets of his testimony, however, something about it leaves us a bit unsettled, doesn't it? It's the money. His eagerness to submit everything to God can leave us questioning our willingness to do the same.

Can we all just assume that upon waking that pivotal day, Zacchaeus had no thought, no inclination, nor even the *possibility* of the joyful generosity for which he is now known? Money was his master—the insatiable god of a calloused life— for this tax collector had amassed his fortune by gouging others, rising as faithfully as the morning sun to pursue still more by detestable means. Yet on *this* day, his mind was elsewhere: "He wanted to see who Jesus was,"[23] and by nightfall, he had. Zacchaeus called Him "Lord!"[24] and with everything he had, he would serve his new God, the true God.

Jesus once observed, "How hard it is for the rich to enter the kingdom of God!"[25] yet of his wealthy host He declared, "Today salvation has come to this house."[26] How did this

---

[23] Luke 19:3
[24] Luke 19:8
[25] Luke 18:24
[26] Luke 19:9

happen? What moved Zacchaeus to choose this new path in the opposite direction? In Jesus, he had encountered an engaging God who knew his name and desired his

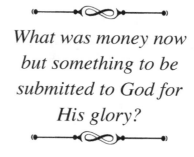

What was money now but something to be submitted to God for His glory?

company. In Christ, he had met a humble God who suffered from the crowd a rejection He did not deserve in order to show mercy to this man whose rejection was well earned. On mission to see who Jesus was, Zacchaeus found that Jesus knew *him* well and that He had come to seek and to save *him*, "the lost."[27] He had seen who Jesus was, and he "received him joyfully."[28] What was money now but something to be submitted to God for His glory?

Transformation begins with "Christ in you, the hope of glory."[29] His Spirit moves in us, softening our hearts awakened by love, sharpening our minds to know what is true, and strengthening our wills "to work for his good pleasure."[30] Jesus is worth far more than anything we have; we can trust Him with everything we are.

Father, I cannot fathom all You have done for me, but I can praise You for it. Change my heart into one that does as You

---

[27] Luke 19:10
[28] Luke 19:6 ESV
[29] Colossians 1:27
[30] Philippians 2:13 ESV

lead me to do, submitting everything to You, always in gratitude and joy. Be my Lord. In Jesus' name I pray. Amen.

Section Two

The Samaritan Woman

S he had a name; I wish we knew what it was. Instead she is known by the six-syllable sobriquet, "the woman at the well," or its seven-syllable substitute, "the Samaritan woman." We know some things about her, and we speculate perhaps too much about others. Some say she was promiscuous, though some suspect barren; whatever the cause or combination of causes, when she encountered Jesus, she'd had five husbands and was living with a man out of wedlock. Her lonely trek for water in the midday sun suggests some level of rejection by the townsfolk, yet when she ran back to them with news about a prophet, they believed her. Also, shamed or not—or to whatever degree—when the Jewish man spoke to her, breaking at least two social mores in the process, she responded not timidly, but in direct (if not entirely truthful) conversation.

Perceiving Jesus to be a man of understanding and authority, the woman took refuge at times in the safety of traditions, citing her ancestors' place of worship and the legacy of their community well, for instance. There is something compelling about a greater revelation, however, that frees us from paradigms of the past, and it was not long until the Samaritan woman hurried back to her town of Sychar, teeming with hope. "Come, see a man who told me everything I ever did. Could this be the Messiah?"[31] she called out, perhaps blessing in the process some who had been unkind to her. The love of Christ frees us this way.

The story of Sychar is not only the remarkable transformation in this woman through her encounter with Jesus but also the change in the villagers who heeded her call to come and see Him for themselves. Taking Him at His word without demanding any miraculous proof of His authenticity, they said to their neighbor, "We no longer believe just because of what you said; now we have heard for ourselves, and we know that this man really is the Savior of the world."[32] Her impact is legendary. Though we do not yet know her name, we will one day, for surely it is written in the book of life. So, too, are those of many from the town of Sychar, for in proclaiming Jesus to others, the Samaritan woman bore the fruit of a new heart. Watch and see.

God uses sinful people to share Good News

---

[31] John 4:29
[32] John 4:42

Something Better

Shortly after they married, my mother and father faced a minor dilemma; it concerned card games. Both of them enjoyed this recreational blend of socializing and strategy, but there was just one hitch: Dad liked pinochle, but Mom enjoyed bridge. Neither had played the other game before, so they agreed to try each one together and then decide which to pursue as a couple. They joined friends for bridge first, and on the way home, my father said, "We can forget pinochle." He would let go of his old pastime, for he had found something better.

It is human nature to favor the familiar; we shed old paradigms only when something superior shines brighter by comparison. Such was the case with the woman at the well. The repartee with Jesus about bodily thirst and social propriety now behind them, her conversation turned to deeper matters of the spirit, and as it did, she scurried for safety to trusted traditions. When He revealed Himself to be the source of living water, for instance, she replied, "Are you greater than our father Jacob, who gave us the well and drank from it himself, as did also his sons and his livestock?"[33] When she perceived herself in the presence of a prophet, she doubled down in discomfort: "Our ancestors worshiped on this mountain, but you Jews claim that the place where we must worship is in Jerusalem."[34]

---

[33] John 4:11–12
[34] John 4:20

People around the globe and throughout time find comfort in their traditions. Yet when these sources of identity become fortresses of retreat and hiding places from truth, we miss the person of Jesus Christ—the purity of His soul, the fullness of His character, and His glorious plans for us. He comes to us "not ... to condemn the world, but to save the world."[35] He engages us in everyday life through activities as simple as a genuine conversation beside an old well. There a woman saw beyond mountains that divide and cities that separate to a unifying place where "true worshipers will worship the Father in the Spirit and in truth."[36] It was enough—she was beginning to change, for she had found something better, and leaving her water jar and paradigms behind,

It was enough—
she was beginning
to change, for
she had found
something better...

she went to tell others about Jesus. Her witness continues today, assuring us He will engage us, too, as we leave the safety of our old ways and trust in the One who secures us in Himself.

Father, we are humbled before the Samaritan woman's openness to Jesus, Your Son. Grace us also to leave behind any comfortable thing that would keep us from trusting entirely in Him. In His name we pray. Amen.

---

[35] John 3:17
[36] John 4:23

It Is What It Is, or Is It?

I t was yet another family member trip to the hospital, which
of course portended more medical bills in the mailbox. His
circumstance unchangeable, my friend sighed in disgust, "Oh
well, it is what it is." Overhearing him from the other room, his
wife called back in a more optimistic tone, "But it's not what it
will be!" Pithy and profound, her rejoinder was just the encouragement he needed to hear. They've retold the story often in the
ensuing years, always to the delight of their listeners.

For the woman at the well, "It is what it is," was well-
known at the time and remains well-chronicled today. By her
own account, her very existence had begun two social rungs
below that of the tired and thirsty stranger seated before her and
seeking her help. "You are a Jew and I am a Samaritan woman,"
she replied, "How can you ask me for a drink?"[37] Living with
a man not her husband, a fact she tried to conceal, dropped her
another frustrating step down to defeat in a real-life game of
Chutes and Ladders. Surely this was not the "happily ever after"
of her earlier dreams, *nor was it the fullness of Jesus' plan for
her.* For she was the first to whom He revealed Himself as the
Messiah: "I who speak to you am he,"[38] Jesus told her. And
from unsearchable depths, He offered her "living water,"[39] a

---

[37] John 4:9
[38] John 4:26 ESV
[39] John 4:10

"spring of water welling up to eternal life,"[40] that would forever quench the thirsting of her soul. "Sir, give me this water,"[41] she accepted. Her "is what it is" was no longer; her "what it will be" had come.

We tend to view the Samaritan woman as she was on her way to the well that day, but this is not the same person who returned to her town, nor would she ever be that person again. The Messiah changes things, and not merely so, for He makes us new. "If anyone is in Christ," proclaimed Paul, "the new creation has come: The old has gone, the new is here!"[42] Our sin patterns no longer define us—this is true of the woman who left the well; it is true also of us. We have met the Messiah, and we, like her, are new; we are different than when we came. Let no one persuade us otherwise.

Father, thank You for making me a new person in Christ. Help me to trust Your faithfulness, goodness, and eternal care as You continue to make me like Him. In His name I pray. Amen.

---

[40] John 4:14
[41] John 4:15
[42] 2 Corinthians 5:17

An Honest and Good Heart

There is good news we welcome, there is exciting good news we share, and then there is teeming good news, the kind that rises up and spills over our well-polished containers of propriety. What, though, hastens us as heralds of good news even to our antagonists, those who exclude us with cold shoulders, judge us with pointed fingers, or dehumanize us through indifference? What raises us to a place higher than pride, purer than resentment, and stronger than fear? Grace does.

Her destination was a well—a pit, she called it—perhaps an apt metaphor for a life of deepening failures and darkening hope, and she was there to draw still more, yet again. This noonday, though, grace awaited her there, an appointment set before the beginning of time. She, like so many through the ages, had awaited the Messiah—"When he comes, he will explain everything to us,"[43] she said—and now He was there, seeking from her a drink from the pit and offering living water from an inner well—a spring, He called it—sourced in Himself and rising up to eternal life. She came to the well bogged down by her failures and left it as one uplifted in grace. Teeming with good news and unable to contain it, she returned to her villagers, including her detractors there, saying, "Come, see a man who told me everything I ever did. Could this be the Messiah?"[44] What confidence! What purpose! Such transformation!

---

[43] John 4:25
[44] John 4:29

Grace is like that: it sends us spilling over with good news of undeserved favor. Freedom is like that: it releases us in relief with the proclamation of pardon. Jesus is like that: He flows from us like streams of living water, even to those who don't love us. He rises up in hearts made new in Him, people "who have heard the word in an honest and good heart, and hold it fast, and bear fruit with perseverance."[45] And if fruitfulness is its measure, I think we can safely say the Samaritan woman went back to her people with a new heart, "an honest and good heart." For as John writes, "They came out of the town and made their way toward him."[46]

At times, we don't *feel* new, but if in faith we drink from the "spring of water welling up to eternal life"[47]—Jesus Christ himself—we *are* new, and our failures define us no more. Ours is to embrace what is true, rest in Him who makes us new, and with honest and good hearts, persevere. The fruit will be there; He will see to it.

Father in heaven, Your Spirit lives in me through faith in Christ. Grace me to go and bear fruit with an honest and good heart. Amen.

---

[45] Luke 8:15 NASB
[46] John 4:30
[47] John 4:14

A Sprig Grows in Sychar

Frank Mickes was an inmate at Marion Correctional Institution (MCI) when Christine Money became its warden. Until that turning-point, the place was "drug-infested, gang-infested, and on the verge of rioting, a bad situation to be in as a young man," recounted Frank, now a few decades older and free. But Mrs. Money brought to MCI a new approach, one from, in his words, a heart "driven by God." She invited inmates to attend a Kairos Prison Ministries weekend, 42 men at a time, and the population soon began to see change—"a feeling of inner freedom" is how Frank describes it today. The new warden also lived out her Christian faith inside the prison, listening, caring, acting, and building trust. Over time, MCI became known among Ohio's incarcerated community as "God's house."

We have been celebrating a Samaritan woman made new by grace before the compassionate Christ—hope dispelling disillusion, honor replacing shame, and joy overcoming pain. Yet her personal change was only the beginning of a larger and lasting legacy, for her story surpasses herself. Made new in the power of grace, she returned to her people in the boldness of freedom, heralding Messianic hope. John narrates their precious response: "They came out of the town and made their way toward him."[48] No commentary is needed, for the remarkable scene speaks for itself. "I tell you," Jesus said to His disciples

---

[48] John 4:30

21

as they watched, "open your eyes and look at the fields! They are ripe for harvest. Even now the one who reaps draws a wage and harvests a crop for eternal life."[49]

Does anything demand our attention as much as a life made new? It sounds a triad of good news in gentle tones to the soul: Jesus is real; He lives today; there is hope! So it was that the Samaritans of Sychar came and heard for themselves this man who claimed to be the Christ. To the woman they said, "We no longer believe just because of what you said; now we have heard for ourselves, and we know that this man really is the Savior of the world."[50] From one person's change a community was transformed. Then who knows what our impact might be when we tell of our own encounters with Christ? We may think our testimonies to be ineffective, but the Spirit of God works through them to spread grace, stir hope, and speak life all around us. People will be changed, and God will be praised. Be willing, be eager; speak, and watch.

Lord God, change us for a purpose—to trumpet new life and to glorify You. Shine through Your people, and draw others to Yourself, where they will find fullness of life in Your Son. In Jesus' name, Amen.

---

[49] John 4:35–36
[50] John 4:42

Section Three

Naomi

O n the shelves of Old Testament works, wedged between the larger tomes of Judges and 1 Samuel, stands the beautiful little book of Ruth. The work is entirely contained in four brief chapters, its spine not wide enough to bear its name, its small size belying its timeless power and depth. From a literary perspective, it is a brilliantly written short story, yet there is nothing fictional about it, for its epilogue shows Ruth to be the eventual grandmother of David, Israel's greatest king. We know the story primarily as the "redemption" of its widowed namesake, and as such a prophetic telling of our own redemption through her progeny, Jesus Christ, the Son of God. Yet the pages of Ruth also tell the heartening story of transformation, that of her mother-in-law. Her name was Naomi.

To Naomi and her family, seeing was believing, and practicality meant self-reliance. Amid famine they emigrated to Moab, leaving the promised land, perhaps doubting the faithfulness of Him who had promised it to His people in the first place. When Naomi's husband and two sons died, she urged her daughters-in-law to return to their people, again citing the insurmountable barriers to her own ability to provide. In doing so, she came dangerously close to sending away Ruth, through whom God would show Naomi His unshakeable presence and sustaining love, and draw her to trust in Him.

We were made to rest in God and to receive His comfort through people who care.

We cannot control everything, though our sinful nature would try, nor do all solutions depend on us. We were made to rest in God and to receive His comfort through people who care. This then would be Naomi's journey—a painful one, for sure—yet one that would mercifully escort her from emptiness to fullness, from helplessness to happiness, and from distress to security. She would emerge from the illusion of self-sufficiency and rest in the kindness of others; she would burst forth from her barricades of bitterness and live in the sustenance of God. She who had accused God as the source of her misery would now praise Him from the depths of her transformed heart. Naomi means, "pleasant," which is what she became—pleasant, again. Watch and see.

The Good in Grief

My son recently asked me, "Why do you work out as much as you do?" "So I can do the things I do at my age," I replied. Later, the *real* reason returned to mind—I began a regimen decades ago, determined to spare my family from the bitter agony of loss. My own father had died suddenly and prematurely, leaving his young family emptied of his presence, lacking his provision, and longing for his love. How could I let my wife and son experience such pain? I would stay fit and ask God for long life.

The Old Testament book of Ruth is a beautiful short story of redemption—the rescue from loss and restoration to fullness at a cost borne by another. Yet the account is every bit as vivid a depiction of inner transformation, in this case that of Ruth's mother-in-law Naomi, by way of the painful path that wends through grief. Losing her husband and two sons had rendered Naomi bitter and blaming: "The Almighty has made my life very bitter. I went away full, but the LORD has brought me back empty."[51] Most of us have been there ourselves, and we have stood beside many Naomis in our life, speaking the soft words of a silent presence.

Yet in His sovereignty, God commands even death to serve His good purposes for our lives, for grief brings us to an unavoidable encounter with real thoughts and deep feelings

---

[51] Ruth 1:20–21

now exposed before us. We appreciate more fully the unique beauty of those now gone, though frustrated we cannot proclaim it in their presence. Left behind, we carry the heavy load of unresolved guilt, or we lay it before God in the cleansing power of confession. We find our love was stronger than we had known, and perhaps our hurts deeper. We draw nearer to God in reliance on Him, or we distance ourselves in resentment. And in the clarity of loss, God is there, meeting us wherever we are, eager to embrace, patient to wait and faithful to heal.

And in the clarity of loss, God is there, meeting us wherever we are, eager to embrace, patient to wait and faithful to heal.

The apostle Paul wrote that suffering produces perseverance, character, and hope,[52] and in the context of suffering he penned the familiar verse, "in all things God works for the good of those who love him."[53] But these are words more apt for another day. For now, Naomi sobs, she questions; survival is aspiration enough. And though we will not say today what she cannot hear today, we know this to be true—that God is at work in her even now, commanding her pain to work for her good.

Father, there is no sting worse than death; sustain us in our grief. Strengthen us to persevere, command our pain to build

---

[52] Romans 5:3–4
[53] Romans 8:28

our character, and sustain us in the sure and certain hope of eternal life through Jesus Christ, our Lord. In His name we pray. Amen.

Night Lights

We were visiting at the kitchen table when my mother shared with me a pattern she had observed both from her own experiences of grief and those of others. "When we lose someone we love, there is usually a strong support network for about three months," she said. "People call, stop by, and bring food, but after three months, they think things are better, so they resume life as normal. But things are *not* OK; we're *still* hurting, and now we're hurting *alone*." Mom continued, "I've learned to wait three months and then step in to offer help when one's support is beginning to fade." The candle of care, lit by others, still flickers kind rays of hope.

It is hard to imagine the darkness of the widow's anger or the depth of her pain. "Don't call me Naomi [pleasant]," she said, "Call me Mara [bitter], because the Almighty has made my life very bitter."[54] *Heap more hurt on me. Call me "bitter" whenever you look upon me. Remind me what God has done to me and who He has made me to be—bitter.* What can one possibly say to heal invisible wounds of unknown depth? Whose words are wise enough? Solomon writes, "Like one who takes away a garment on a cold day, or like vinegar poured on a wound, is one who sings songs to a heavy heart."[55]

Consider then the heart and wisdom of Ruth, widowed herself at a young age. To her grieving mother-in-law, she offered not

---

[54] Ruth 1:20
[55] Proverbs 25:20

28

Band-Aids of bromides but the kindness of commitment—perhaps the only words Naomi could absorb. "Where you go I will go, and where you stay I will stay. Your people will be my people and your God my God. Where you die I will die, and there I will be buried."[56] *I am with you.* Then with actions of integrity, Ruth provided for the two of them by humble means—"Let me go to the fields and pick up the leftover grain behind anyone in whose eyes I find favor." "Go ahead, my daughter"[57]—Naomi's heart, healing.

Blessed are those who refuse to let our bitterness and pain overcome us, who reconcile us to hope when we are wary of hope. Awesome are they who sacrifice their lives to save ours with a love that transforms us and a grace that sustains us to a new day of reawakening. When the time comes for us, the comforted, to comfort others, may we be found committed to care, to bearing their burdens and sacrificing ourselves for them.

*Carry each other's burdens, and in this way you
will fulfill the law of Christ. (Galatians 6:2)*

Father, thank You so much for those who have sustained me through the darkest moments of life. They are a gift. Grace me to be as faithful when I am called to do the same. In Christ I pray. Amen.

---

[56] Ruth 1:16–17
[57] Ruth 2:2

Renewed with Fresh Purpose

t happens not infrequently—as I ring the bell for The Salvation Army at Christmastime, someone approaches the iconic red kettle with a recognizable humility. They mine their billfold for money and gladly tuck their gift of gratitude into the slot. Then with a long-ago look in their eyes and the familiar smile of fond recollection, they say something like this: "I remember when I was a child and our family was in tough times. The Salvation Army was there for us." Healing acts of kindness change us— though we remember the isolating pain of emptiness, it is the Christlike character and care of others that fill us, sustain us, and send us down a new path of fresh purpose.

Overwhelmed by the deaths of her husband and two sons, Naomi had tried to send her daughters-in-law away: "Return home, my daughters. Why would you come with me?"[58] One did return to her people, but Ruth remained, displaying the truly noble character for which she would become known— loyal, respectful, compassionate, practical, and industrious—a reputation reaching people's ears even before her visage met their eyes. Said Boaz to Ruth upon their first encounter, "I've been told all about what you have done for your mother-in-law since the death of your husband—how you left your father and mother and your homeland and came to live with a people you did not know before."[59] He saw to it, then, that she would be

---

[58] Ruth 1:11
[59] Ruth 2:11

protected and honored in his fields as she picked the sheaves the harvesters had left behind. Her kindness kindled his own, though neither had an inkling where this shared trait might take them.

But Naomi did! Boaz was a relative of her late husband, and under Jewish law, he could "redeem" Ruth from a life of want and emptiness by marrying her. And Naomi knew it. *Raison d'être! Fresh purpose! Put me in, Coach, I got this!* "My daughter," said the elder to the younger, "I must find a home for you, where you will be well provided for. Now Boaz, with whose women you have worked, is a relative of ours... Wash, put on perfume, and get dressed in your best clothes. Then go..."[60] Ruth had been all about Naomi, and now the reawakening Naomi would be all about Ruth.

God "comforts the downcast."[61] He "comforts us in all our troubles, so that we can comfort those in any trouble with the comfort we ourselves receive from God."[62] Then even our mourning has meaning, growing us into a people who give comfort as only the comforted can give. And so sculpted into the character of Christ, we go forward with fresh purpose—to be there for others in their troubles. They wait for us, hoping. We go to them, caring. Blessed be the name of the Lord.

Father, thank You for those You have sent to comfort us—we need them. Bless them. Heal us in our hurt, and send us to

---

[60] Ruth 3:1–3
[61] 2 Corinthians 7:6
[62] 2 Corinthians 1:4

others as conduits of Your healing and hope. In Jesus' name I pray. Amen.

Fuller Fullness

A friend of mine is fond of saying, "When you reach the end of yourself, you come to the beginning of God." Though we like to think ourselves sufficient in our wisdom and ways, life has a way of proving otherwise. Striving produces riches that don't enrich, willpower is openly mocked by addictions, mortality stirs at dreaded diagnoses, and one person cannot sustain a relationship alone. For Naomi and her family, self-sufficiency meant living by sight and not by faith. Amid famine, they left the promised land for seemingly greener pastures, and when Naomi's husband and two sons died, she assessed the situation within the confines of her own abilities, urging her daughters-in-law, "Return home, my daughters. Why would you come with me? Am I going to have any more sons, who could become your husbands?"[63] And who was God but someone to blame? "I went away full," Naomi lamented, "but the LORD has brought me back empty."[64]

Yet she would know His love. She would experience it through Ruth, her daughter-in-law, who in the words of Naomi's friends, "loves you and who is better to you than seven sons."[65] God's love would shine through Boaz, whose integrity and compassion would bring redemption and closure: "The LORD bless him!" said Naomi to Ruth, "He has not stopped

---

[63] Ruth 1:11
[64] Ruth 1:21
[65] Ruth 4:15

showing his kindness to the living and the dead."[66] She would touch and feel God's love through the grandchild laid in her lap and through the celebratory cry from the women of the town: "Naomi has a son!"[67] No longer would they call her "Mara" (bitter); she was renewed, she was *Naomi* again.

It hurts to lose those we love; it stings like nothing else possibly can. Yet God uplifts us with the present hope of a greater glory, "an inheritance that can never perish, spoil or fade ... kept in heaven for you."[68] It is the Father's will for us, expressed through the Son's prayer for us: "Father, I want those you have given me to be with me where I am, and to see my glory, the glory you have given me because you loved me before the creation of the world."[69] It is in this confidence that we are transformed to become to those who follow us as those who came before us, people who comfort and care—people like Ruth, Boaz, and now, Naomi.

Lord, Your Spirit transforms us in beautiful ways through the lovingkindness of others. Renew us and fill us, that we would become emptied of self and useful to those who, like us, need Your comfort and care. In Jesus' name, Amen.

---

[66] Ruth 2:20
[67] Ruth 4:17
[68] 1 Peter 1:4
[69] John 17:24

Section Four

Jacob

"I've learned not to trust anyone who doesn't walk with a limp," my friend Dennis quipped. I chuckled at his comment, delivered in a tongue-in-cheek sort of way, but not entirely, for we had been discussing the genuine change God patiently brings about in people through their own brokenness. Both of us had seen it; both of us had experienced it. My friend's allusion, of course, was to Jacob, whose life had been one of self-serving deception, getting what he wanted when he wanted it and by means of his own guile. Human relationships were to him expendable, and as far as he was concerned, God was the God of his father Isaac and his grandfather Abraham, but not his own. Jacob acknowledged the Almighty One, but as little more than a source of otherwise unattainable blessing and One with whom to bargain.

Jacob was the kind of son who breaks a parent's heart and the kind of brother who makes his siblings fume. Many would give up on someone like this and feel justified in doing so, but

God loves the unlovable, and His patience goes to extremes. Using the consequences of Jacob's own selfishness and introducing into his life an equally cunning father-in-law, God waited decades as Jacob exhausted under the weight and futility of his scheming ways. Then in an all-night struggle reflecting life-long strife, an angel of God dislocated Jacob's hip, thereafter the source of his limp. It was Jacob's turning point.

If Zacchaeus shows us change can be immediate, Jacob is living proof that transformation into the image of Christ also takes time, a long time—in fact a lifetime. For every loved one who has ever strayed, there is Jacob, who holds out hope. For every remorseful one who feels it is too late in life to be changed, there is Jacob to prove otherwise. For those who believe in the Savior but wonder if they'll ever "get it right," Jacob's life testifies to the tireless work of God in the human heart. For in the patience and kindness of God, Jacob became broken. The God of his fathers was now his God too. Watch and see.

God Waits

Meet Jacob. If ever there were a man whose name fit his disposition, it was he—Jacob means "deceiver," and what an accomplished deceiver, he was! Add schemer, for good measure. He callously commandeered his older brother's birthright, diabolically duped his unseeing father into giving him the blessing of the firstborn, and he absorbed his father-in-law's wealth while managing his flocks. "Isn't he rightly named Jacob?"[70] fumed Esau, his twice-bested twin. Jacob even bargained with God, offering, "If God will be with me and will watch over me ... so that I return safely to my father's household, *then* the LORD will be my God."[71]

Deception and scheming declare in devilish tones: *my desires are more important than your wellbeing*. People are means to our ends, expendable if it comes to that, and injustice is merely collateral damage. "All's fair in love and war," we blithely chirp. What we do not realize when we manipulate and mislead others is that treachery and lies ultimately isolate us—like Jacob fleeing a vengeful Esau and decades later a cheated Laban, we run away from the consequences of our actions or live in fear of them. Even if we remain, we live at arm's length from once trusting, now cynical victims; though present in proximity, their wounded trust, or what's left of it, has moved on. There we exist, alone with our spoils.

---

[70] Genesis 27:36
[71] Genesis 28:20–21, emphasis added

Yet our scheming is no match for God's character. "If we are faithless, he remains faithful"[72]—this is His nature, and He will not waver from it; even in affront He will not be moved from His redeeming love. He speaks the wise counsel of conviction into our soul, and He allows the repercussions of our actions to take their toll—all that we might set aside our conniving ways and turn to Him for newness of life. Paul wrote, "Don't you see how wonderfully kind, tolerant, and patient God is with you? Does this mean nothing to you? Can't you see that his kindness is intended to turn you from your sin?"[73] Yes, in tireless kindness, God waits for the Jacobs of this world to tire of control and to rest in His wisdom and ways, for our well-being is His desire.

Father, how good You are! Even my worst will not change Your best. Lead me away from my controlling ways; strengthen me to trust You and to rest in Your wisdom, sovereignty, power, and love. Amen.

---

[72] 2 Timothy 2:13
[73] Romans 2:4 NLT

Mirror, Mirror

At some point along the way, I came to realize the more I dislike certain character flaws in others, the more likely it is I am seeing in them a mirror image of my own unsavory traits. How deflating this was to discover! But over time I have come to embrace these "reflection experiences" as steps in the transformation process, humbling revelations of my need for confession, correction, and growth. In this way, God uses even sins—both those of others and our own—and their consequences to expose our shortcomings and to weary us of our will. This is precisely where we find Jacob: having deceived his father into giving him the blessing of the firstborn son, he fled its rightful recipient, Esau, who had sworn to kill his scheming sibling. Jacob escaped his brother, only to encounter a man who, over the next twenty years or so, would emerge as his doppelgänger in deception and every bit his equal—Laban. Let the games begin.

Jacob had offered to work seven years for Laban in exchange for permission to marry his daughter Rachel. Hidden under the wedding veil, however, was Leah, the older daughter, who Laban thought should marry first! "*Why have you deceived me?*"[74] demanded Jacob. Laban ultimately honored his promise of Rachel's hand in marriage, but only "in return for another seven years of work."[75] Said Jacob, tiring, to Laban, "Send

---

[74] Genesis 29:25, emphasis added
[75] Genesis 29:27

me on my way so I can go back to my own homeland ... You know how much work I've done for you."[76] Laban prevailed once again, however, convincing Jacob to stay and tend his flocks, but this time Jacob got the upper hand, scheming a way to deplete his father-in-law's wealth while building his own. When Jacob "noticed that Laban's attitude toward him was not what it had been,"[77] he fled again, now a humbler man. "If the God of my father, the God of Abraham and the Fear of Isaac, had not been with me," said Jacob to Laban, who had pursued him, "you would surely have sent me away empty-handed. But God has seen my hardship and the toil of my hands, and last night he rebuked you."[78] Jacob's guile had failed him, but the God of his fathers had not.

"There's a divinity that shapes our ends, Rough-hew them how we will,"[79] wrote Shakespeare. Though God created us to thrive under His blessing and to be a blessing to others, we are drawn to ways and means that serve us first and most, but never best. Yet even in our rebellion, God commands the consequences of our decisions to show Himself faithful and to bring us to grace, "that we might not rely on ourselves but on God."[80] Jacob reached this point. Have we?

---

[76] Genesis 30:25–26

[77] Genesis 31:2

[78] Genesis 31:42

[79] Shakespeare, William. *Hamlet. The Oxford Shakespeare*, edited by Stanley Wells and Gary Taylor, (New York: Oxford University Press), 685.

[80] 2 Corinthians 1:9

Jacob

Father, Your love for me never changes. Thank You! Do what You must to draw me to Yourself, that I would rely completely on You. Grace me to trust and obey. In Jesus' name I pray. Amen.

Committed

When she taught high school, my mother had one particularly unruly student—you know, the one who pushes the limits, seemingly daring others to reject him, while inwardly hoping someone won't. His antics were unacceptable, of course, so Mom occasionally made him stay after school in detention, where he challenged her even more. "But I saw something in him," she recalled years later, "and I wasn't going to take the bait." Over time, he began to trust her acceptance, and his behavior started to change. Following graduation, he pursued what would become a productive lifetime career in the armed services, and when he came home on leave, he would visit my mother and thank her for not giving up on him.

Just as He did for Abraham and Isaac, God promised rich blessings to Jacob, but what his father and grandfather humbly received in trust, Jacob selfishly seized by treachery—helping himself to the blessings while rejecting the God who gave them.

He will not compromise His character in reaction to any antics we can devise...

It is the kind of brazen behavior that infuriates us and compels us to sever relationships now, completely, and forever. But "God cannot be tempted by evil,"[81] and

---

[81] James 1:13

He will not compromise His character in reaction to any antics we can devise, however plentiful or diabolical they may be. We can wrestle against Him all we want, as Jacob did, but His love for us will not wane; if anything, our combativeness only accentuates His patience and faithfulness. So Jacob wrestled alone with God, an unavoidable moment of truth. Their struggle lasted a nighttime but reflected a lifetime, and when daylight broke, so did Jacob—his hip wrenched and his name changed. He was no longer Jacob (deceiver), but Israel (he struggles with God), because he had "struggled with God and with humans and [had] overcome."[82]

Self dies hard. We all wrestle with God, to different degrees perhaps, and each of us in our own way. So it is by God's

We overcome because He never gives up on us.

grace that we eventually come to see the self-centered life for what it is—"hostile to God"[83] and "contrary to the Spirit."[84] Yet God remains true to His people and committed to His promises. "The LORD your God is God," said Moses to the people gathered before him, "he is the faithful God, keeping his covenant of love to a thousand generations of those who love him and keep his commandments."[85] God sees something in us—a

---

[82] Genesis 32:28
[83] Romans 8:7
[84] Galatians 5:17
[85] Deuteronomy 7:9

creation in His image—and though we struggle with Him, He remains unchanging in character and unwavering in love. We overcome because He never gives up on us.

Father, thank You for being true to Your word and tireless in love. May we cease from our struggles against You and rest entirely in You, for this is Your desire for us. You are good to Your people and faithful to Your promises. In this confidence and in the name of Jesus we pray. Amen.

Lifelong Learning

James Thornton is a friend of mine; we attend a Bible study together and work out at the same fitness facility. One day I mused to James, a captive audience on the treadmill at the time, "Isn't it frustrating, the fact that we learn so many important things late in life, things that would have made life so much better had we only known them sooner?" A seasoned smile spread across his face as he slowly shook his head. "No," he replied, "it tells me God has more things for me to do here, so He's still working on me. He's teaching me new things for a reason." James was right: God never stops molding us for our good and equipping us for His purposes.

Through a life of strife, Jacob shows us the reality that coming to love and trust God takes time, and being transformed into His image even longer. It is not natural to set aside our will for God's ways; rather it is the tireless work of His Spirit that changes us through lifelong care. This is to the glory of God and to our favor, for it illumines the depth of sin from which we have been saved and magnifies the wonder of His patience, even as He forms this trait in us. "The Lord is not slow in keeping his promise, as

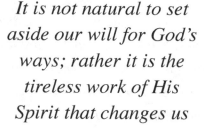

It is not natural to set aside our will for God's ways; rather it is the tireless work of His Spirit that changes us through lifelong care.

some understand slowness. Instead he is patient with you, not wanting anyone to perish, but everyone to come to repentance,"[86] wrote Peter. The pace of change that seems to us so painfully slow is to God quite purposeful—He molds each of us at a tempo that turns us safely to Himself.

To Jacob, God had been the God of his fathers, but not his own. So God waited as Jacob, over time, suffered under the consequences of his foolish decisions and limited power. Having run from Laban and now toward Esau, both of whom he had cheated, Jacob began to understand the futility of his ways and to embrace the character of a holy God. "O God of my father Abraham, God of my father Isaac ... I am unworthy of all the kindness and faithfulness you have shown your servant ... Save me, I pray ... for I am afraid."[87] God remained true to His promises, and after Jacob had reconciled and found favor with his two adversaries, he set up an altar and named it not after the God of his old name, Jacob, but the God of his new name, Israel. He had become a beautifully broken man and useful for God's purposes, for the God of his fathers was now the God of Israel too.

Father, I confess You transform me not on my timeline, but Yours. You know what You are doing in me, and what You are doing in me is good. Thank You. Be my God, and help me rest in You as You steadily transform me into the likeness of Your Son. In His name I pray. Amen.

---

[86] 2 Peter 3:9
[87] Genesis 32:9-11

Section Five

Thomas

Thomas' friends called him Didymus, and perhaps John did so more than the others, for whenever he mentioned Thomas in his gospel, he appended his nickname, which means "the twin." We know nothing about Thomas' anonymous sibling; in fact, if it weren't for John, we would not know much about Thomas either, for the other three gospel writers merely list him as one disciple on a roster of twelve. Yet we do know this about the man: he was there. At the Sermon on the Mount, he was there; when Jesus sent His disciples out in pairs to preach the good news and heal the sick in His name, the twin was there, and he saw much. For three years, John was there, too, and would one day record for us some crucial moments in the life of this relatable man.

We know him today as "doubting Thomas," yet to limit him to a single defining adjective would be a disfavor not only to him but to ourselves as well. Haven't we all been tempted to doubt, and does our sin define us today? Thankfully it does not; our identity is in Christ. Thomas showed himself to be the kind of person whose desire to gain understanding compelled him to seek clarity, as on at least one occasion he was the only one bold enough to ask it from Jesus. He was honest as well, even if in an inglorious form, as when being candid about one's own doubts.

We can appreciate and even admire Thomas' deep desire for wanting only what is right and true, and one's caution not to misstep is wise. Sometimes, however, "just one more" question or condition is, at its core, our insistence that belief in God remain on our terms or that He, like us, is not always to be trusted. But God *is* faithful; He patiently coaxes us from the confines of our natural senses and gently leads us in the freedom of faith to fullness of life in a kingdom not of this world. Watch and see.

Thanks for Asking

O ur company had hired John from a nearby competitor, and as he and I got to know each other, we discovered we knew some people in common, including Tom. I had met Tom a few times at industry events, but John had worked with him daily as managers for the same employer. "What I really respect about Tom," John began, "is the fact that, no matter how many people are in a meeting, he is unafraid to admit that he doesn't understand something, and he will continue to ask questions until he does." Before this point, I could be counted among the timid souls who preferred to sit quietly in ignorance rather than risk the embarrassment of revealing it, but I immediately decided to take courage from this story of Tom's honesty and henceforth to pursue a matter until I understood it.

Encouraging His disciples in His final hours, Jesus said, "I will come back and take you to be with me that you also may be where I am. You know the way to the place where I am going."[88] We are left to wonder about the blank stares, the unconvincing head-nods, and the length of unknowing silence before Thomas audibly confessed what surely all silently wondered: "Lord, we *don't* know where you are going, so how can we know the way?"[89] He had been one of the quiet disciples, but in this moment the world needed someone willing to set aside personal pride to gain eternal truth—the world needed

---

[88] John 14:3–4
[89] John 14:5, emphasis added

Thomas. For Jesus' answer to his question has echoed for millennia, stating a sure and certain claim that will never cease to be true: "I am the way and the truth and the life. No one comes to the Father except through me."[90]

We call him "doubting Thomas," but I think we could just as easily think of him as "honest Thomas." Understanding and certainty were so vital to him that he stepped into the momentary leadership vacuum, speaking courageously and seeking clarity, not content to be without it. Aren't we glad! Yet Thomas will learn more—much more—in the next two weeks of his life, for as important as it is for us to seek knowledge and truth, we must also reach the point of trusting what we do not see or cannot fully comprehend. It is called faith—being sure of Jesus in whom we hope, Him who, as we now know, is the way and the truth and the life. We come to the Father through Him. (*Thanks for asking, Thomas!*)

Father, thank You for hearing us when we seek to understand You and for speaking truth to our soul—Your Word is truth. Strengthen us to live this life by faith in Your Son who loves us and gave Himself up for us. In His name we pray. Amen.

---

[90] John 14:6

Two Words

"Don't be afraid; just believe."[91] —*Jesus, to Jairus*

S teve was sharing some personal life struggles with his friend Ray, when Ray surprised him with a question, "Have you ever really asked Jesus into your life?" Caught a bit off guard, Steve replied that he had been a church goer all his life, but Ray persisted: "But have you ever really committed to Him?" Ray then shared with Steve a prayer to receive Jesus as his Savior, which Steve took with him to consider further on his own. A couple of weeks later, Ray asked Steve if he had prayed this prayer. "Yes," he replied, "but I don't feel any different." With a smile on his face, Ray said two words that would change everything for Steve: "Just believe."

As a disciple of Jesus, Thomas had seen much in the past three years: miracle after miracle, healing after healing, and the dead raised to life. He had heard much along the way: parable after parable, Scriptures explained, and the future foretold. Thomas himself had even participated in miracles and teaching, for he had been among those sent out in twos, going "from village to village, proclaiming the good news and healing people everywhere."[92] But when his friends enthusiastically proclaimed their eyewitness report of Jesus' resurrection from

---

[91] Mark 5:36
[92] Luke 9:6

the dead—"*We have seen the Lord!*"[93]—Thomas said to them, "Unless I see the nail marks in his hands and put my finger where the nails were, and put my hand into his side, I will not believe,"[94] his adamance perhaps as telling as the refusal itself.

As we approach the precipice of belief, new obstacles to faith emerge and old ones loom larger. Broken promises in our past make it difficult to trust fully today. Other belief systems confuse us, making us wonder which one is true or dulling us into the indefensible notion that all of them are. Losing control is always a fear, and relinquishing it to One we cannot see is even more so. And sometimes we are deceived into doubting we can be forgiven. We do well to carefully consider our way, of course, for actions have eternal consequences (as does inaction), yet in this life there will always be one more question, one more objection, or one more fear. So we seek God in prayer and His Word, and we pursue understanding, but for each of us, full and forever life in Christ ultimately comes down to two words that change everything: "Just believe."

Father, belief can be difficult for me as, in fear and pride, I struggle at times to relinquish control and to rest in You. Send Your Spirit to give me the grace and strength to trust in Your love and walk in Your ways. In Jesus' name I pray. Amen.

---

93 John 20:25
94 John 20:25

A Moment and a Lifetime

During my teenage years, many of my friends found a deeply satisfying faith in Jesus Christ. Personally, I believed God existed and mentally assented to Christian teaching, but whatever rest my friends had found in Christ, I had not. How deeply I longed for the inner peace and joy that emanated from their souls! So I kept coming back. To Bible studies, I kept coming back. To church, I kept coming back. To seeking God through prayer, I kept coming back. It would be ten long years of "coming back" before I trusted in Jesus' love and forgiveness, and in retrospect, it has become clear that Jesus was drawing me all along from unbelief to belief. "I, when I am lifted up from the earth, will draw all people to myself,"[95] He had promised, and over time I found His promise to be true.

It had been eight days since Thomas rejected his friends' testimony of Jesus' resurrection—"Unless I see ... I will not believe,"[96] he had vowed. Yet when Jesus appeared to them a second time, Thomas was with them; though unbelieving, he had kept coming back. Perhaps he sensed the inner peace and joy emanating from his friends and yearned for it himself, but whatever the reason, it was Jesus faithfully drawing Thomas to Himself. "Reach here with your finger, and see My hands," He

---

[95] John 12:32 ESV
[96] John 20:25 NASB

told his unbelieving disciple, "and reach here your hand and put it into My side."[97] *Just trust me, Thomas.*

🌿 Whether ten years, eight days, or a lifetime, the vital journey from unbelief to belief in Jesus covers the same immeasurable distance, for it is the path from our ways to God's ways, from false notions and deceptions to Him who is true, and from eternal separation from God to eternal life in His Son. Then belief is not a one-time event, but rather the continuing essence of the life reborn in Christ: "Do not *be* unbelieving, but believing,"[98] Jesus' words to Thomas still resound to us today. And when we do believe, we are "included in Christ [and] marked in him with a seal, the promised Holy Spirit, who is a deposit guaranteeing our inheritance until the redemption of those who are God's possession."[99] This is God's promise and the Spirit's work in all who live in Christ through faith, people like Thomas, who now proclaimed before his risen Savior, "My Lord and my God!"[100] Thomas found His promises to be true; Thomas had become a believer.

My Lord and my God, draw me to Yourself. Call me always from unbelief to belief, for You are who You say You are: the way, the truth, and the life. Grace me to rest in You. Amen.

---

[97] John 20:27 NASB

[98] John 20:27 NASB, emphasis added

[99] Ephesians 1:13–14

[100] John 20:28 NASB

One More Beatitude

o doubt Thomas knew a beatitude when he heard one. In the Sermon on the Mount, Jesus had declared rich blessings for those who pursue God's ways amid the hardships and temptations of life: theirs is the presence of inner joy and the promise of divine provision. Now having shown Himself to this hold-out disciple who would believe in His resurrection by no other means, Jesus added one more beatitude—"blessed are those who have *not seen* and yet have believed."[101] It was the definition of faith: "the assurance of things hoped for, the conviction of things *not seen*."[102] It seems so counterintuitive, doesn't it, that we who believe without seeing are the ones who are blessed! Why is *"not seen"* such a vital part of our journey; why does God prize faith so highly among us and infuse it with joy?

When we trust only what we see, we believe on our terms and subject God to our demands, but faith forsakes our reign and submits to what is true—the sovereign rule of God. It is how Mary, perplexed at the news she would give birth to the long-awaited Messiah, nevertheless replied, "I am the servant of the Lord; let it be to me according to your word."[103] Conditional belief doubts God's character, as though He were like us, not always to be trusted. But faith rests securely in God's goodness,

---

[101] John 20:29 ESV, emphasis added
[102] Hebrews 11:1 ESV, emphasis added
[103] Luke 1:38 ESV

wisdom, power, and love, as did Sarah, who "by faith … received power to conceive, even when she was past the age, since *she considered him faithful who had promised*."[104] Then also, if "God is spirit,"[105] how can we grasp Him with natural senses that live only to see the grave? In faith, however, we view the unseen through the clarity of the gospel sent "to open [our] eyes, so that [we] may turn from darkness to light and from the power of Satan to God, that [we] may receive forgiveness of sins and a place among those who are sanctified by faith in [Jesus]."[106]

> *Faith moves us from our kingdom to God's kingdom, from our power to His power, and we look upon His glory even as we share in it.*

Faith—itself "the gift of God"[107]—is, in Peter's words, "more precious than gold."[108] We can see why! Faith moves us from our kingdom to God's kingdom, from our power to His power, and we look upon His glory even as we share in it. Peter continues, "Though you have not seen [Jesus], you love him. Though you do not now see him, you believe in him and rejoice with joy that is inexpressible

---

104 Hebrews 11:11 ESV, emphasis added
105 John 4:24
106 Acts 26:18 ESV
107 Ephesians 2:8
108 1 Peter 1:7 ESV

and filled with glory, obtaining the outcome of your faith, the salvation of your souls."[109] Blessed are we, indeed, who see through the eyes of faith.

> *Yours, O LORD, is the greatness and the power and the glory and the victory and the majesty, for all that is in the heavens and in the earth is yours. Yours is the kingdom, O LORD, and you are exalted as head above all. (1 Chronicles 29:11 ESV)*

---

[109] 1 Peter 1:8–9 ESV

Section Six

Peter

The brothers were from Bethsaida near the Sea of Galilee, fishermen by trade. Andrew had been a disciple of John the Baptist—"the voice of one crying out in the wilderness, 'Make straight the way of the Lord'"[110]—and perhaps Peter had been too. Yet when Jesus of Nazareth came along the seashore, saying "Follow me," both of them dropped their nets and did so. Of the two brothers, and ultimately of the twelve disciples, Peter was the leader. Whenever the gospel writers mentioned several of them by name, his was listed first among them. An external processor, and an extreme one at that, Peter was the kind of person who blurts his thoughts aloud in real-time while others ponder matters in the more private quarters of the mind. Also, if he owned an inner "pause button" to interrupt the flow between event and reaction, it had a faulty connection, for at times his quickness to speak and to act bypassed sound

---

[110] John 1:23 ESV

judgment. Still, his impetuousness sparked conversations and established the premises from which they commenced, leaving it to others to affirm, refute, or forfeit their opportunity to speak.

Like all of us, Peter had admirable character traits about him: boldness, decisiveness, and proactivity, to name a few. But he also had his flaws, and because of the excesses of his nature—we could insert *"very"* before any of his descriptors—his flaws seem exaggerated, perhaps making it easier for us to admit our own. We see clearly in his story what we must confront in ourselves: we are unspiritual by nature, and everything about us must be brought under the lordship of Jesus Christ by the power of His Spirit in us. The strength of self-will does not equate to the power of God's Spirit; in fact, "these are in opposition to one another,"[111] so no matter how hard we try, we in our flesh cannot please God. We can only please the Father by trusting in the Son with whom He is eternally well pleased.

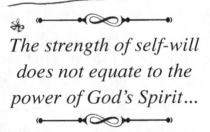

The strength of self-will does not equate to the power of God's Spirit...

What lay ahead for Peter is what lies before for us as well—the relinquishment of pride, the donning of humility, the refusal to fear, and the courage to trust—none of which we can accomplish or attain on our own, but all of which we find in Christ. What we take from Peter, then, is not comfort in his foibles

---

[111] Galatians 5:17 NASB

but confidence in his God, who in patience abided Peter in his flesh, while in love filling him with His Spirit. Watch and see.

Peter's Very Bad Day

Have you ever had one of those days when seemingly nothing transpired the way you had hoped? Of course! We all have. How much worse are calamities of the self-inflicted variety, when pride prevents us from admitting our limitations, accepting correction from others, or reaching out to them for help. Consider, then, Peter's very bad day. On arguably the most pivotal night in human history, this disciple refused to let Jesus wash his feet, naively vowed unequaled loyalty, argued when foretold otherwise, slept when commanded to pray, and severed the ear of the high priest's servant—all before denying Jesus three times! "And he went outside and wept bitterly."[112] Who wouldn't? Peter had experienced Spirit-led moments before— for example, when confessing Jesus to be "the Messiah, the Son of the living God"[113]—but this was not one of them.

It is easy to point to Peter's flaws and somehow feel better about ourselves by comparison, or to find curious relief in a misery-loves-company sort of way. His failures, though, serve as real-life reminders of the human condition we share, for we are by nature "unspiritual"[114]—unwilling and unable to lead a godly life in our own wisdom and strength. The apostle Paul's confession could just as well have been Peter's and ours: "I know that nothing good dwells in me, that is, in my flesh. For

---

[112] Matthew 26:75
[113] Matthew 16:16
[114] Romans 7:14

I have the desire to do what is right, but not the ability to carry it out."[115] Without the Spirit, our mind is "hostile to God, for it does not submit to God's law; indeed, it cannot. Those who are in the flesh cannot please God."[116] No, we can find no relief in Peter's perils, for the fact that they parallel our own exposes all of us and exonerates no one.

A wiser Peter, long since restored, wrote that "[Jesus'] divine power has given us everything we need for a godly life through our knowledge of him who called us by his own glory and goodness. Through these he has given us his very great and precious promises, so that through them *you may participate in the divine nature*, having escaped the corruption in the world caused by evil desires."[117] The hope we take from Peter, then, is in his God, for God does not abandon us to the hopeless task of changing our sinful nature as if we were capable of fixing ourselves through steely resolve. In His mercy, rather, He makes our fleshy failures work for our good by proving the opposite, that we cannot be spiritual in our own power, no matter how strenuously we exert it or how "saintly" we disguise it. Then how much more is God glorified, for in great love He forgives us of our pride and fills us with the Spirit, that through Him we will live effectively and productively in the divine nature of Christ, and cease striving in our own. This is His heart; this is His doing in us. Praise His name.

---

[115] Romans 7:18 ESV
[116] Romans 8:7–8 ESV
[117] 2 Peter 1:3–4, emphasis added

Father, You are good, and You seek only good for us. Deliver us from the temptation to live in our own wisdom and strength and thus avoid You. Fill us instead with Your Spirit to draw us near, that we may follow where He leads us. We pray in the name of Christ. Amen.

Restored

We had heard inmates share life perspectives that only the incarcerated could gain, but the prison ministry volunteers were unprepared for what this man had to say. "What I did was wrong, and I'm serving my sentence for it. But how would you like for your *entire life* to be judged by your worst decision on the worst day of your life?" We caught our breath; we understood. We had all experienced "worst" decisions and days and would prefer they not define us.

Peter had grievously erred. Shortly before His betrayal, Jesus had warned his disciples they would soon desert Him, citing Zechariah's centuries-old prophecy, "I will strike the shepherd, and the sheep of the flock will be scattered."[118] Yet Peter asserted his resolve above God's Word and his allegiance beyond that of the others, insisting that "though they all fall away because of you, I will never fall away."[119] He scattered like everyone else, of course, and of the Twelve only Peter denied knowing the Lamb of God—not once but thrice—surely the worst decision on the worst day of his life. Would this tragic moment define Peter? Is this how he would be forever judged?

In Christ Jesus, what appears to us as a defining point of sin and death becomes for us the turning point of truth and grace. When he appeared to His disciples for the third time after His resurrection, Jesus purposefully engaged Peter, not to condemn

---

[118] Matthew 26:31 ESV
[119] Matthew 26:33 ESV

him but to restore him—to mend this broken disciple and to send him whole again into a meaningful life of work for His kingdom. Peter had brazenly proclaimed unequaled loyalty to Jesus, but now when Jesus asked Peter if his love for Him exceeded that of the others, the humbled disciple avoided comparison, saying only, "Yes, Lord; you know that I love you."[120] Peter had denied Jesus three times, and three times Jesus asked him, "Do you love me?" At each "Yes," Jesus pointed Peter to the divine call of proactive love: feed my sheep; take care of them.[121] What a relief forgiveness is, and how refreshing are new beginnings!

We need not be defined by our worst decisions and days, for Jesus has overcome them, and all who live in Him by faith are made new.

We need not be defined by our worst decisions and days, for Jesus has overcome them, and all who live in Him by faith are made new. We stand in the truth of forgiveness and serve in the freedom of grace, knowing this assurance from Peter, who learned it first-hand himself: "After you have suffered a little while, the God of all grace, who has called you to his eternal glory in Christ, will himself restore, confirm, strengthen, and establish you."[122]

---

[120] John 21:15 ESV
[121] John 21:15-17
[122] 1 Peter 5:10 ESV

As He does, our trust in the flesh fades, and our love for God grows. Jesus defines us now, for we live *all* our days in Him.

Father, thank You for new life in Christ, in which our sin defines us no more. Strengthen us and send us to serve in Your humility and for Your glory, however You call us to do this today. In Jesus' name, Amen.

You Will Receive Power

> *"Fellow Israelites, why does this surprise you?*
> *Why do you stare at us as if by our own power*
> *or godliness we had made this man walk?"*[123]
> —Peter, to the gathering crowd

The transformation in Peter was clear. The disciple who fearfully denied knowing Jesus to "one of the servant girls of the high priest"[124] had come to speak boldly of the resurrected Christ to the crowds and even to the high priest himself. This impulsive disciple who had brashly pledged unparalleled loyalty to Jesus had come now to understand where godly greatness lies: "Humble yourselves, therefore, under God's mighty hand, that he may lift you up in due time."[125] The reactionary who once cut off the servant's ear in defense of Jesus had now healed a lame man in His name. How could this man's life have changed so completely?

Hours before His betrayal, Jesus spoke peace to his troubled friends. "Unless I go away the [Holy Spirit] will not come to you," He explained, "but if I go, I will send him to you."[126] This "advocate," He said, would be given "to help you and be

---

123 Acts 3:12
124 Mark 14:66
125 1 Peter 5:6
126 John 16:7

with you forever,"[127] adding that "the Spirit of truth ... will be in you."[128] The Son of God had come, as promised, to be *with* us for a season and for a purpose, and now to all who would receive Him by faith, He promised an even closer presence, a lasting unity: the Spirit of God will be *in* you forever.

"If Christ is in you," wrote Paul, "the Spirit gives life because of righteousness."[129] The indwelling of "the Spirit of Christ"[130] is life itself; likewise, it is essential to our transformation into His image and our effectiveness in His name. We flourish when we understand this. It is so vital, in fact, that three times Paul implored the Corinthians to grasp its truth. "Do you not know ... that the Spirit of God dwells in you?"[131] "Do you not know that your body is a temple of the Holy Spirit who is in you?"[132] "Do you not recognize this about yourselves, that Jesus Christ is in you?"[133] We become like Jesus not as people trying to become better versions of our old selves, prone as they are to pride and fear, but as people born of the Spirit into Christ, submitting to His presence in us, and living in this "new self, created after the likeness of God in true righteousness and holiness."[134] Christ is our life, and we become more like

---

[127] John 14:16
[128] John 14:17
[129] Romans 8:10
[130] Romans 8:9
[131] 1 Corinthians 3:16 NASB
[132] 1 Corinthians 6:19 NASB
[133] 2 Corinthians 13:5 NASB
[134] Ephesians 4:24 ESV

Him as we submit ourselves to His Spirit in us. As we humble ourselves in faith before Him, He will do great things through us, His people.

Father, thank You for making us new in Christ. Fill us with Your Spirit, that in humility we would submit all to You today, living and serving in the confidence of Your presence and power. In Jesus' name we pray. Amen.

Three Steps Forward

A s a young man newly promoted to a field representative position for my employer, I traveled with my manager as he introduced me to the insurance agents who sold for our company throughout north central Ohio. We had plenty of "windshield time" together over a several week period, so I was privileged to learn from his time-tested cache of workplace wisdom, including this valuable observation: "Some people gain twenty years of experience one time, and others gain one year's experience twenty times." It was his warm way of setting for me a vision of constant learning, continual growth, and increasing productivity. In a similar vein, Peter counseled believers that life in Christ is more than a single moment of salvation—it begins at our spiritual birth into Him and grows steadily through a lifelong process of maturing. "The God and Father of our Lord Jesus Christ," he wrote, "... has caused us to be *born again into a living hope* ... to an inheritance that is imperishable, undefiled and unfading, kept in heaven for [us]."[135] God's Spirit births our spirit to a purposeful existence of learning and serving, all toward the vision that we "grow up in [our] salvation"[136] and "bear much fruit."[137]

Yet amid the three-steps-forward adventures along the way, there arise some one-step-back moments of frustration. They

---

[135] 1 Peter 1:3–4 ESV, emphasis added
[136] 1 Peter 2:2
[137] John 15:5

happen to all of us; they happened to Peter. He had come to terms with the spiritual weakness of his natural self, experienced the relief of his restoration, and availed himself to the Holy Spirit, who had done much in and through this bold apostle. Yet when influential people began to argue the need to attain righteousness by keeping Jewish law, even Peter was intimidated and "began to draw back and separate himself"[138] from Gentile believers. It took a public rebuke from Paul to disabuse Peter of his misstep into doubt and to realign him with the truth of salvation by faith in Christ alone.

Shortly before his martyr's death, Peter penned some final three-steps-forward thoughts to "those who through the righteousness of our God and Savior Jesus Christ have received a faith as precious as ours."[139] "Make every effort," he wrote, "to add to your faith goodness ... knowledge ... self-control ... perseverance ... godliness ... mutual affection ... and love. For if you possess these qualities in increasing measure, they will keep you from being ineffective and unproductive in your knowledge of our Lord Jesus Christ."[140] By now we know we cannot bear such spiritual fruit in our natural strength but only when we offer ourselves entirely to the leading of the Spirit of God. Though we stumble backwards here and there along the way, we can be confident in this: He will call us ever-forward

---

138 Galatians 2:12
139 2 Peter 1:1
140 2 Peter 1:5–8

in constant learning, continual growth, and increasing productivity—a lifetime of transformation, one time.

Father, show us Your will, and grow us in wisdom, so our life would be pleasing to You. Grace us to rely on—and to be productive through—the power of Your Spirit and to endure all things in patience and trust. We give You thanks, for You are good. In Jesus' name we pray. Amen.

Section Seven

Joseph

W e have heard of family dynasties before, but none like the one into which Joseph and his brothers were born. To the three generations of patriarchs immediately preceding them, the God of the universe had promised rich blessings, and through them He vowed to bless humankind for all time. On occasion, God would even identify Himself by these ancestors' names: *the God of Abraham, Isaac, and Jacob*. One would think this would be an ideal family—generous, caring, and kind to all they met—but then one would be wrong. Rather, with a sordid history of deceit, incest, thievery, prostitution, assault and murder, this clan was reality TV material long before its time. Imagine then what might happen when into this volatile mix enters a father's favorite son, born late in life to his favorite wife—a kid brother named Joseph.

To look at his life from a human perspective (only God can peer into the heart), we would call Joseph a good guy. He had his little brother moments, certainly, and probably worse, but by our standards he was at least stalwart in integrity, inclined toward the right thing, and reliably faithful to God. Even "good people" suffer at times from the free will decisions of others, however, and for years Joseph would incur injustice after injustice, all stemming from one such decision of his brothers—to sell him into slavery in a different land. Though God was faithful, commanding Joseph's trials ultimately to work to his favor, the man had been wronged and had much to forgive. He tried, instead, to forget.

In this Biblical account, we see God's radically transforming power through forgiveness, both that which we extend to others and that which we receive from them. For as Joseph tried improbably to suppress the pain of wrong, his brothers tried impossibly to carry its guilt. They could do neither. Their metamorphosis, then, was a shared one—the confession of truth and the joy of release, the healing from hurt and the presence of peace. In the mercy of God, Joseph and his brothers became reconciled. Watch and see.

Joseph

The Isolation in Rejection

What causes fights and quarrels among you?
Don't they come from your desires that battle
within you? (James 4:1)

His brothers' feelings toward him were intense, and not in a good way, for "they hated him and could not speak a kind word to him."[141] So when Joseph dreamed of them bowing down to him, "they hated him all the more,"[142] then after voicing their disdain, they hated him yet *"all the more."*[143] He'd had his bratty moments, such as tattling on them to their father, but sibling comeuppance usually fits the indiscretion, so what could possibly drive his brothers to plan Joseph's murder before opting instead to sell the seventeen-year-old into slavery? In a word, *favoritism.* Their father Jacob was partial to Joseph, his favorite son from his favorite wife, which was a measure of rejection for his brothers and ultimately an unfairness to Joseph, for any imprudence on his part, however mild, became an accelerant to the resentment raging in their soul.

Sin separates. James tells us the divisions among us emerge from the desires within us. Envy resents others for their good fortune, and there is distance. Lust objectifies its targets, indexing their inherent value to our impulsive desires, and

---

[141] Genesis 37:4
[142] Genesis 37:5
[143] Genesis 37:8, emphasis added

there is contempt. Rage bursts our inner restraints to lash out at others, lest our fragile pride be toppled or our deepest fears realized, and accusations presume to know the heart of another. In a me-first world, unity is unnatural, and harmony easily broken, so human trafficking would not be the last injustice Joseph suffered. In fact, it portended his suffering through a steady stream of wrongs—attempted assault, false witness, wrongful imprisonment, and abandonment—that, over the next thirteen years, would sweep him further into relational isolation.

Most of us have not experienced the degree of injustice that Joseph suffered, but sin—both that which we inflict and that which we endure—has brought us discord and division. Whether we've retaliated against others or retreated within ourselves, whether we've shut out or shut down, unity has become a casualty. Yet here we take courage from the story of Joseph, for despite his circumstances, "the LORD was with Joseph,"[144] not in the sense of delivering him from difficulties, but in a far more powerful way—by humbling him through his trials and leading him through reconciliation, and in the process, blessing Joseph for God's higher purposes and our greater good. It is in this love that God calls us, as well, to the humble way that leads us out of isolation and unto reconciliation, oneness, and God's good pleasure.

Father, You love me beyond measure or understanding. In this comfort, may I gratefully and humbly walk the supernatural

---

[144] Genesis 39:23

path to reconciliation and restoration through Jesus Christ, in whom "all things hold together."[145] In His name I pray. Amen.

---

[145] Colossians 1:17

The Admission in Suppression

E arly in his college career, our son Matthew initiated a pattern of calling Peggy and me every Sunday afternoon, catching up with each of us for a half hour or so before going his merry way. This was a welcome development from one who, in his high school years, communicated chiefly in monosyllabic grunts at the dinner table! So great did these regular weekend conversations feel to this parent that I began to call my mother each week as well, a Friday appointment we kept—this weekly gift of touch—for over ten years until she passed away.

Have you noticed Joseph never called home? Despite all the abuses he suffered, Joseph rose to become second-in-command over Egypt, so how easy would it have been for one in his position to send a note to Dad, saying, "all is well" or "stop by and see me sometime"? How smugly gratifying it might have been to send a portrait-hieroglyph to his brothers, wryly signed, "in command and thinking of you." No, he never called home, but then why would he? The past was to him something to be left behind and forgotten. He named his first son Manasseh (forget), saying, "It is because God has made me forget all my trouble and all my father's household,"[146] and his second, Ephraim (twice fruitful), saying, "It is because God has made me fruitful in the land of my suffering."[147] Suppression—in

---

[146] Genesis 41:51
[147] Genesis 41:52

his case, forgetting without forgiving—was Joseph's way of moving forward.

While Joseph carried the pain of yesterday's wrongs, his brothers bore the burden of their unresolved guilt. In trouble before the high-ranking Egyptian official—Joseph, whom they failed to recognize—their long-muted consciences found voice among themselves: "Surely we are being punished because of our brother. We saw how distressed he was when he pleaded with us for his life, but we would not listen; that's why this distress has come on us."[148] The inevitable blame-shifting that followed came from Reuben: "Didn't I tell you not to sin against the boy? But you wouldn't listen!"[149] (*Not helpful, Reuben.*)

Whether of pain or guilt, suppression is unhealthy and overwhelming. In fact, it is misleading, for our ongoing attempts to bury our past betray our inability to resolve conflicts alone. Paul urges us instead to "call home" and resolve the wrongs among us God's way: "Bear with each other and forgive one another if any of you has a grievance against someone. Forgive as the Lord forgave you."[150] Confession that leads to forgiveness and reconciliation—this is the truthful, liberating way of Christ, and He calls us to it.

Father, forgiveness can be difficult for me when pride, fear, and resentment get in the way, yet I deeply desire Your higher, liberating ways. Grace me with the love, strength, and freedom

---

[148] Genesis 42:21
[149] Genesis 42:22
[150] Colossians 3:13

to forgive. In the name of Christ and the power of Your Spirit I pray. Amen.

From Confession to Unification

Peggy and I were touring the city of Belfast, Northern Ireland, an opportunity that, given the long-entrenched strife between Protestants and Catholics there, would have seemed improbable but for the "Good Friday Agreement" signed a little more than a decade before our visit. We viewed the dry dock where the *Titanic* was built—"She was alright when she left here," the locals will say—and as we drove along beside a section of the city's "peace wall," someone in our group asked, "What's on the other side of that wall?" It was a tourist question, for sure, and though our driver maintained his composure, there was a distinct tone of incredulity in his one-word response. "Catholics!" he exclaimed. We stifled our smiles before redirecting our thoughts to the sobering matter of peace by separation.

Reconciliation takes guts, for the real battle lies within, where fear cowers within a seeming fortress of pride. Seeing his brothers for the first time in over twenty years, Joseph could have dismissed from his presence these he had purposed to forget; instead, he skillfully led them on the more difficult journey toward a more glorious destination—forgiveness and oneness. He tested his brothers by recreating scenarios similar to those in which they had once failed him: the opportunity to abandon a brother, favoritism toward the youngest, and the declaration of intent to enslave one of their own, in this case Benjamin. Judah implored in response, "If my father, whose life is closely bound up with the boy's life, sees that the boy isn't there, he will die... Now then, please let your servant remain here as my lord's slave in place of the boy, and let the boy return with his brothers."[151] This sacrificial act in humility was, for Judah and the others, a tacit confession of their past wrongs. All eyes turned to the Egyptian ruler.

"I am Joseph! Is my father still living?"[152] he cried, no longer able to contain himself. Before his speechless brothers, Joseph "wept so loudly that all the Egyptians [in his household] heard him."[153] And as his sobs purged Joseph of his pain, he released his brothers from their guilt. "Do not be distressed and do not be angry with yourselves for selling me here; because it was to save lives that God sent me ahead of you."[154] "He kissed all his brothers and wept over them. Afterward his brothers talked with him."[155] Theirs was no longer the mere absence of external conflict, but the mature peace of reconciliation that emerges from hearts made humble.

> *Reconciliation with each other is as important as our reconciliation with God, for there is no room for separation in the body of Christ.*

---

[151] Genesis 44:30–34
[152] Genesis 45:3
[153] Genesis 45:2
[154] Genesis 45:5
[155] Genesis 45:15

The apostle John wrote, "Whoever claims to love God yet hates a brother or sister is a liar. For whoever does not love their brother and sister, whom they have seen, cannot love God, whom they have not seen."[156] Reconciliation with each other is as important as our reconciliation with God, for there is no room for separation in the body of Christ. He draws us to unity in Him.

Father, as You have forgiven me of all my wrongs against You, humble me and guide me to forgive those who have hurt me. This is Your good and perfect will; strengthen me to obey You. In the name of Him who bore my sin I pray. Amen.

---

[156] 1 John 4:20

The Glory in Reconciliation

We had reached an impasse. My corporate team had analyzed performance trends and was revising our insurance pricing structure in one of our states, a joint effort we pursued with the office managers responsible for daily operations in the region. Opposing opinions led to fomenting frustrations, and though I knew we would reach an agreement, I reported our stalled status to my manager, who offered this helpful piece of advice. "When negotiating, don't approach the matter as though across the table from an adversary, but from the same side of the table as though confronting a common enemy shoulder to shoulder." We were, after all, teammates facing the same outside competition and sharing the same internal goals.

Self-interest blinds us to the greater good; we are "lured and enticed by [our] own desire"[157] and lose sight of God's will and ways. How beautiful, instead, when we peer beyond our worldly skirmishes and behold our sovereign God actually pursuing His kingdom purposes *through us*, undeterred by our pettiness. Once Joseph's identity was revealed to his brothers who had badly mistreated him, he sought not divisive retribution but the shared understanding of a higher plan. "God sent me ahead of you to preserve for you a remnant on earth and to save your lives by a great deliverance,"[158] he said. Joseph realized that, in His sovereignty, God had turned sibling infighting

---

[157] James 1:14 ESV
[158] Genesis 45:7

toward their own good and His own glory, for in Egypt this entire family found not only immediate relief from devastating famine but also an incubator of sorts in which they and their offspring would grow into a great nation under the protection of a world power. Israel would emerge from Egypt 400 years later as foretold, "a community of peoples"[159] to possess the land promised to Abraham, Isaac, and Jacob. And through this lineage the Messiah would enter human history to save people from all nations and reconcile us to God.

God is glorified in unity. Though we were "alienated from God and ... enemies in [our] minds because of [our] evil behavior," God has "reconciled [us] by Christ's physical body through death to present [us] holy in his sight, without blemish and free from accusation."[160] This is God's desire for us; it was Jesus' prayer for us: "I have given them the glory that you gave me, that they may be one as we are one—I in them and you in me—so that they may be brought to complete unity."[161] We go, then, as one reconciled people—"Christ's ambassadors"[162]—carrying this living, breathing message: "that God was reconciling the world to himself in Christ, not counting people's sins against them... Be reconciled to God."[163]

---

[159] Genesis 48:4
[160] Colossians 1:21–22
[161] John 17:22–23
[162] 2 Corinthians 5:20
[163] 2 Corinthians 5:19–20

Working in Us What Is Pleasing to Him

> *How good and pleasant it is when God's people*
> *live together in unity! (Psalm 133:1)*

Father, thank You for uniting us to Yourself and to each other in Christ. Even as we grow as one in Him, send us as ambassadors with the proclamation of forgiveness, reconciliation, life, and love in His name. Amen.

Section Eight

Cornelius

ornelius was not the first centurion Peter had encountered; there had been another. The faith of the one had left Jesus astonished; the faith of this man would lead to a world changed. As an officer over 100 soldiers, Cornelius respected authority and understood trust—whether keeping peace or fighting wars, both are critical to success. Devout, God-fearing, and generous, he was respected by the Jewish people, no easy accomplishment for a Gentile officer in Rome's military machine. He knew *about* Jesus and knew that peace could be found in Him and that He "went around doing good and healing all who were under the power of the devil, because God was with him,"[164] but he did not *know* this Messiah, at least not yet.

Like pieces from opposite corners of a puzzle, Cornelius and Peter—an officer and a fisherman—converged toward each other, snapping into place in an emerging kingdom map.

---

[164] Acts 10:38

God had long declared his purpose that His people, Israel, be a "light for the Gentiles."[165] and Jesus had commissioned His disciples to be "witnesses in Jerusalem, and in all Judea and Samaria, and to the ends of the earth."[166] In Cornelius' home in Caesarea, then, this Gentile received Israel's "light." The pieces connected; the breach closed.

It is God's deep desire that we be changed into the image of Christ; this is the work of His Spirit in us. Yet it is also God's plan and provision that we who have been divided in the flesh be united now with each other in the body of Christ. This, too, is transformation as we build each other up "until we all reach unity in the faith and in the knowledge of the Son of God and become mature, attaining to the whole measure of the fullness of Christ."[167] It is good and right that the life-stories of Cornelius and Peter converged—the Jew and the Gentile, united now in Christ who has made in Himself "one new humanity out of the two."[168] Watch and see.

---

[165] Isaiah 42:6
[166] Acts 1:8
[167] Ephesians 4:13
[168] Ephesians 2:15

New Life

When my friend Scott and I caught up with each other over a lunchtime bowl of chili, we covered the conversation gamut as usual, from our families, to leadership, to what we were learning along life's journey. At one point in our free-flowing conversation, Scott shared this observation—"I think of people as having three lives: our public life, our private life, and our secret life." The profundity of his insight struck me like a jolt. Scott was right: we all showcase what we want others to see in us, reserve what we choose to reveal to but a few, and hide that which we resolve to show no one. As I pondered my friend's comment that day, I recalled from my childhood a Sunday liturgy in which we acknowledged our sin against God "not only by outward transgressions, but also by secret thoughts and desires which I cannot fully understand, but which are all known unto thee." It was a healthy confession of our human nature.

A centurion in the Italian Regiment, Cornelius was a Gentile and a Roman, a demographic that normally drew both political and spiritual scorn from the Jews of his day, yet this was a man "respected by all the Jewish people."[169] His public life and his private life were admirable and aligned, for "he and all his family were devout and God-fearing; he gave generously to those in need and prayed to God regularly."[170] Even an angel

---

[169] Acts 10:22
[170] Acts 10:2

appearing to Cornelius affirmed his integrity, saying, "Your prayers and gifts to the poor have come up as a memorial offering before God."[171] We would call him a "good man," yet something was missing from the humble centurion's life. For there is a difference between knowing *about* Jesus and actually *knowing* Him, and while Cornelius and his family greatly honored God, to them He was external—beheld but not indwelled.

> *We would call him a "good man," yet something was missing from the humble centurion's life.*

"Send to Joppa for Simon who is called Peter," the angel commanded Cornelius. "He will bring you a message through which *you and all your household will be saved.*"[172]

Transformation begins at salvation. Paul writes of this grace: "When the kindness and love of God our Savior appeared, he saved us, not because of righteous things we had done, but because of his mercy. He saved us through the washing of *rebirth* and *renewal* by the Holy Spirit, whom he poured out on us generously through Jesus Christ our Savior, so that, having been justified by his grace, we might become heirs having the hope of eternal life."[173] As Peter spoke in Cornelius' home the gospel story of Jesus' sacrifice, atonement,

---

[171] Acts 10:4
[172] Acts 11:13–14, emphasis added
[173] Titus 3:4-7, emphasis added

resurrection, and authority, "the Holy Spirit came on all who heard the message."[174] The "good man" had become a new man—as had his family and friends—"a new creation"[175] born of the Spirit into Christ. The same must be for all of us, for in Christ Jesus all of our sins—be they "outward transgressions" of the public and private variety, or the thoughts and desires we know well enough to keep secret yet "cannot fully understand"—are washed away. In this security, our transformation into His likeness begins, for spiritual growth in Christ begins at spiritual birth in Christ. Praise His name.

Father, I confess my sins, which are all known unto You. Thank You for forgiving me in Your great love and through Your great sacrifice. In Christ, I am new—this is my confidence; this is my joy. Change my heart to be like Him. In His name I pray. Amen.

---

[174] Acts 10:44
[175] 2 Corinthians 5:17

Tear Down This Wall

The young couple was engaging in good-natured banter when one turned to this bystander and asked, "Whose side are you on?" It was a light-hearted moment, and one teeming with opportunity. "There are no 'sides,'" I replied, "There is only one side, and that is the two of you." (*Whew! A narrow escape.*)

In Peter's culture, there were indeed two sides: Jews and everybody else (or "Gentiles" for short). In their zeal to rise above the *ways* of the world, God's chosen nation had come to regard other *people* of the world as "unclean" and to be avoided. This was never God's intent, so through two men — one a Gentile and the other a Jew — He would show all that, in Christ, He had "destroyed the barrier, the dividing wall of hostility"[176] that had improperly stood between these two groups. To Cornelius, God sent an angelic herald bearing a humbling equation: devout, plus God-fearing, plus generous still comes up short of salvation. The solution? "Send to Joppa for Simon who is called Peter,"[177] the angel commanded the centurion. Then as the officer's contingent approached the seaside city, God spoke humility also to Peter, this time through a vision. "Do not call anything impure that God has made clean"[178] He repeated. God was speaking primarily of people, as the Jewish

---

[176] Ephesians 2:14
[177] Acts 11:13
[178] Acts 10:15

apostle would soon confess before his Gentile host: "God has shown me that I should not call *anyone* impure or unclean."[179]

As God makes us one with Himself through Christ, so He also joins us to each other as members of His body. To the Gentiles in Ephesus, Paul wrote, "now in Christ Jesus you who once were far away have been brought near by the blood of Christ. *For he himself is our peace*, who has made [Jews and Gentiles] one... His purpose was *to create in himself one new humanity out of the two*, thus making peace, and in one body to reconcile both of them to God through the cross... For through [Christ] we both have access to the Father by one Spirit."[180] Growing into the character of Christ means drawing closer together in Him, as well, not letting our differences divide us. To this end, Paul calls believers to be "one in spirit and of one mind,"[181] adding, "Do nothing out of selfish ambition or vain conceit. Rather, in humility value others above yourselves, not looking to your own interests but each of you to the interests of the oth-

> *Growing into the character of Christ means drawing closer together in Him, as well, not letting our differences divide us.*

---

[179] Acts 10:28, emphasis added
[180] Ephesians 2:13–18, emphasis added
[181] Philippians 2:2

ers."[182] This is oneness. This is relational evidence of spiritual transformation. For to unite as one in Christ is to grow in Him who "is all, and is in all."[183]

Father, Christ is our peace; this is Your doing. Grace us to grow in Him, becoming one in spirit and of one mind and, in humility and joy, looking to the interests of others. In His name we pray. Amen.

---

[182] Philippians 2:3–4
[183] Colossians 3:11

You're Welcome

H ave you ever seen the welcome mats that read: "Go away"? I'm guessing most are displayed in the spirit of dry humor, although perhaps an occasional curmudgeon really means what it says. Consider, then, this entryway greeting from a bygone age: "No foreigner may enter within the balustrade around the sanctuary and the enclosure. Whoever is caught, on himself shall he put blame for the death which will ensue."[184] And where would one find this "unwelcome mat"? In the Jewish temple of Jesus' day—it warned the "impure" not to step beyond the "court of the Gentiles" and into the inner temple. Rather than being "a light for the Gentiles, that salvation may reach to the ends of the earth,"[185] God's chosen people had instead come to view others as people from whom to be distanced. *Go away!*

How then did Jewish believers respond to the news that the "Gentiles also had received the word of God"?[186] Blame and accusation: "You went into the house of uncircumcised men and ate with them,"[187] they charged Peter. Now, we could stop here and roll our eyes again at the legalists, marginalizing those who had marginalized others, but the apostle pursued unity and

---

[184] Ben Zion, Ilan. "Ancient Temple Mount 'warning' stone is 'closest thing we have to the Temple.'" timesofisrael.com. https://www.timesofisrael. com/ancient-temple-mount-warning-stone-is-closest-thing-we-have-to-the-temple/ (accessed February 18, 2020).
[185] Isaiah 49:6
[186] Acts 11:1
[187] Acts 11:3

understanding. "Starting from the beginning, Peter told them the whole story"[188] of God's command not to consider anyone unclean and the Spirit's sending the apostle to the officer's home. He told them Cornelius, his family, and friends believed the good news of salvation in Christ Jesus and had received the gift of eternal life for themselves. He told the leadership council about the Holy Spirit indwelling the Gentiles in great power and joy, and then in relatable terms, Peter concluded, "so if God gave them the same gift he gave us who believed in the Lord Jesus Christ, who was I to think that I could stand in God's way?"[189] "When they heard this, they had no further objections and praised God, saying, 'So then, even to Gentiles God has granted repentance that leads to life.'"[190] Chalk one up for God's promise given and God's promise kept; then chalk up another for renewed minds and joyful hearts.

God's purpose is to gather and grow one unified people in Christ Jesus. "For we were all baptized by one Spirit so as to form one body—whether Jews or Gentiles, slave or free—and we were all given the one Spirit to drink."[191] Then as we together join God in His work, He takes us on an adventure beyond the borders of our natural understanding with a message for all who would seek God's kingdom through faith in Christ: Come.

---

[188] Acts 11:4
[189] Acts 11:17
[190] Acts 11:18
[191] 1 Corinthians 12:13

Cornelius

The Spirit and the bride say, "Come!" And let the one who hears say, "Come!" Let the one who is thirsty come; and let the one who wishes take the free gift of the water of life. (Revelation 22:17)

Father, You have welcomed us into Your kingdom as people united with Christ and, through Him, with each other. Stir in us, Your people, to live as open invitations to others, that they, too, would enter in His name. Amen.

Our Kingdom in Common

O ver the past several years, my blog readers have taught me something profound: when we direct our hearts and minds to the Word of God, our worldly differences divide us less and our kingdom joy unites us more. Some perch on the political right, while others lodge somewhere left of center, yet when we ponder together the grace and truth of Christ each week, their responses blend in a harmony of gladness to God. These are precious interactions for me, for in Christ the respective generations, perspectives, and ethnicities only enhance the brilliance, beauty, and wonder of the ever-expanding body that is His church. As Paul wrote, "All of you who were baptized into Christ have clothed yourselves with Christ. There is neither Jew nor Gentile, neither slave nor free, nor is there male and female, for you are all one in Christ Jesus."[192] We could add that in Him there is neither CEO nor intern, nor is there red state and blue state, and other divisions come to nothing, for "in Christ we, though many, form one body, and each member belongs to all the others."[193]

Jesus said, "My kingdom is not of this world... My kingdom is from another place."[194] His is a sovereignty in which hope is secure and joy overflows; it is a rule where justice is satisfied and mercy abounds. Where He reigns, His law of love flows in

---

[192] Galatians 3:27–28
[193] Romans 12:5
[194] John 18:36

the power of His Spirit and serves in His character of humility. We are citizens of this kingdom, for "if you belong to Christ, then you are ... heirs according to the promise."[195] Still, we await this realm in its fullness and glory, when "God himself will be with [us]."[196] Paul tells us, "When Christ, who is your life, appears, then you also will appear with him in glory."[197]

This is where we are going, and each day is a measured stride toward unfading joy. We live, grow, and strive together "that the body of Christ may be built up until we all reach unity in the faith and in the knowledge of the Son of God and become mature, attaining to the whole measure of the fullness of Christ."[198] Would we let disagreements on earthly matters divert us from even a moment of enduring effectiveness? Surely our common enemy would delight at the spectacle of division and seize upon the breach on the spiritual battlefield. Instead, may we be like Cornelius and Peter—the Gentile and the Jew, the officer and the fisherman, both of them once-seeking and now-saved—living humbly in this world and productively toward the next. "Let us throw off everything that hinders and the sin that so easily entangles. And let us run with perseverance the race marked out for us, fixing our eyes on Jesus, the pioneer and perfecter of faith."[199] We live and work as one in Him.

---

[195] Galatians 3:29
[196] Revelation 21:3
[197] Colossians 3:4
[198] Ephesians 4:12–13
[199] Hebrews 12:1–2

Father, You have united us in Christ Jesus. Grace us to fix our gaze on Him in all circumstances, for Your kingdom comes. Send Your Spirit to lead us, so Your will might be done in and through Your people today. In the name of Jesus we pray. Amen.

Section Nine

David

The king needed a staff musician to calm him, and with one soundbite, the talent search was over. "I have seen a son of Jesse of Bethlehem who knows how to play the lyre. He is a brave man and a warrior. He speaks well and is a fine-looking man. And the Lord is with him,"[200] answered a servant. It was enough for Saul; go get the shepherd. The king did not know, however, that Samuel the prophet had anointed David as Israel's eventual ruler and that "from that day on the Spirit of the Lord came powerfully upon David."[201] He did everything well, or so it seemed, courageously rescuing sheep from the mouths of both lion and bear and beautifully composing enduring poetry of laureate quality. Above all, David was in God's words, "a man after my own heart; he will do everything I want him to do."[202]

[200] 1 Samuel 16:18
[201] 1 Samuel 16:13
[202] Acts 13:22

Yet the man was human, and people need people. In fact, God works plentifully and mightily through others at times to urge us forward along His path and to nudge us away from the ditches along either side. No one is made to "go it alone," not even this chosen, gifted, and Spirit-filled king. So at three key points in David's life, God sent someone to say to him what he needed to hear: Jonathan, the son of Saul and best friend to David; Abigail, the wife of Nabal; and Nathan, the prophet.

The Bible teaches us not to accept all input from all comers. Job's friends, for instance, had plenty to say to him—and about him—amid his misery, yet as eloquent as their words may have sounded, they displeased God, who said "You have not spoken the truth about me, as my servant Job has."[203] Had Job not interceded to God on their behalf, they themselves would have suffered for their presumption. But "a word spoken in right circumstances"? Ah, it is "like apples of gold in settings of silver."[204] It rescues us from fear and escorts us to courage. It turns us from wrath and leads us to wisdom. It confronts our sin and humbles us to repentance. It rebukes our doubt and strengthens our faith. These are the words spoken to David through people, words that steered him away from the ditches of his sinful nature and urged him forward in the ways of the Spirit. Watch and see.

---

[203] Job 42:7
[204] Proverbs 25:11 NASB

Jonathan Spoke Strength

My friend Greg invited me to join him for a four-mile run after work one afternoon. Now Greg was a marathoner, but let's just say I ran for health, for I inherited my dad's speed— his friends used to tell him they could time him in the 100 with a calendar. So as the two of us set out, Greg ran a shoulder ahead of me. I felt bad for slowing him down, so I picked up the pace, now running a shoulder ahead of him. He, in turn, notched it up a step, and so it went, each of us silently accelerating the both of us for four miles. As we finished, Greg panted, "You set a strong pace; I was trying to keep up with you." "*I* set the pace?" I gasped amid chest-heaves, "I thought *you* were setting the pace! I was trying not to hold you back!" It was a metaphor for life—people inspire others to reach deeper than anyone would alone, for we grow stronger and excel more when we expend ourselves for others and receive the same from them in support of us.

The son of Israel's king, Jonathan showed greater bravery, humility, and wisdom than his father Saul. Yet his greatest attribute, and the one for which he is best remembered, was his love for a friend, which exceeded self-interest. "Jonathan became one in spirit with David, and he loved him as himself."[205] Then for a season in life, these two men ran its demanding race together. Once when pursued by Saul, who in jealously had

---

[205] 1 Samuel 18:1

sworn to kill him, David went to Jonathan and asked, "What have I done? What is my crime? How have I wronged your father, that he is trying to kill me?"[206] "Never!" Jonathan replied. "You are not going to die!" he said, adding, "Whatever you want me to do, I'll do for you."[207] It was the assurance David needed while fleeing the volatile sovereign. The last time David and Jonathan saw each other was an occasion like so many others — Saul seeking to take David's life and Jonathan seeking to preserve it. "Jonathan went to David ... and *helped him find strength in God*."[208]

Friends in Christ help friends in Christ grow strong. Exhorted Paul, "Encourage one another and build each other up."[209] We ought not focus on pleasing ourselves, he said, but "each of us should please our neighbors for their good, to build them up."[210] Whether we run "a shoulder ahead" of our friends for a time, selflessly urging them upward and onward, or it be they outdo themselves for us, let us "encourage one another daily, as long as it is called 'Today.'"[211]

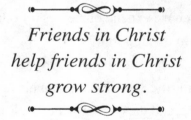

Friends in Christ help friends in Christ grow strong.

---

[206] 1 Samuel 20:1
[207] 1 Samuel 20:2-4
[208] 1 Samuel 23:16, emphasis added
[209] 1 Thessalonians 5:11
[210] Romans 15:2
[211] Hebrews 3:13

Let us speak strength, as Jonathan did, and let us receive strength, as David did.

> *A friend loves at all times, and a brother is born for adversity. (Proverbs 17:17 ESV)*

Father, thank You for those You send to strengthen us. Please bless them, and grace us likewise to encourage others, that they may grow ever-stronger in Christ. In His name we pray. Amen.

Abigail Spoke Wisdom

O ne of the things I enjoy most about prison ministry is that there is not a lot of superficial prattle; rather we talk about hopes and plans, our relationship with God, steps forward and back—real-life issues. Occasionally, the chaplain will remind the residents, *"Remember, your 'best decision' landed you here,"* meaning that what seems like "a good idea at the time," often leads us to a lesser place. Can you remember scenarios, for instance, when "getting even" led to escalation, a harsh word created distance, or lust for something more left us regretting what we lost in exchange? "There is a way that appears to be right, but in the end it leads to death,"[212] and it was in this dead-end direction that David was careening. "Each of you strap on your sword!"[213] he commanded his warriors. Though they had protected Nabal, his servants, and his possessions from Philistine invasion, Nabal foolishly refused the men the provision they needed, returning insult for valor, and now David was marching toward vengeance, well-armed, but not with wisdom. Enter, Abigail, the wife of Nabal.

She was an "intelligent and beautiful woman,"[214] and Nabal's servants knew where to find good solutions. Apprising her of their predicament, one pleaded to her, "Now think it over and see what you can do, because disaster is hanging over our

---

[212] Proverbs 14:12
[213] 1 Samuel 25:13
[214] 1 Samuel 25:3

master and his whole household. He is such a wicked man that no one can talk to him."²¹⁵ Abigail acted quickly, offering sustenance to David's hungry army, then feeding wisdom to his angry soul. Shifting the blame from her foolish husband to her humbler self, she diffused David's wrath, enabling him to divert his attention from Nabal's short-term offense to God's long-term plan, saying, "the LORD your God will certainly make a lasting dynasty for my lord."²¹⁶ Thus reminded of God's faithfulness to him, David was able to hear Abigail's appeal not to sin against God. "When the LORD has fulfilled for my lord every good thing he promised concerning him and has appointed him ruler over Israel," she said, "my lord will not have on his conscience the staggering burden of needless bloodshed or of having avenged himself."²¹⁷

Hers was wisdom from God, and David recognized it. "Praise be to the LORD, the God of Israel, who has sent you today to meet me," David replied, "May you be blessed for your good judgment and for keeping me from bloodshed this day and from avenging myself with my own hands."²¹⁸ David's "best decision" had changed: his sword was sheathed, and his God glorified. A Biblical proverb reads, "Walk with the wise and become wise,"²¹⁹ which was what David did that day—he walked with

²¹⁵ 1 Samuel 25:17
²¹⁶ 1 Samuel 25:28
²¹⁷ 1 Samuel 25:30–31
²¹⁸ 1 Samuel 25:32–33
²¹⁹ Proverbs 13:20

Abigail and became wise. Then let us learn from both of them, she who humbly spoke wisdom and he who humbly received it.

*She speaks with wisdom, and faithful instruction
is on her tongue. (Proverbs 31:26)*

Father, thank You for sending us people who speak godly wisdom. We hear Your voice through their words. Grant us Your wisdom, too, that we would not speak the wisdom of this world but Your words of truth and life. Amen.

Nathan Spoke Truth

"Thou art the man."[220] It was Nathan's signature line (always best delivered in King James English). Through a veiled parable of a rich man pitilessly robbing a poor man of his sole possession—a pet lamb—the prophet had raised David's ire to the boiling point, pouring over in condemnation of such injustice. Only then did Nathan proclaim, *"Thou art the man,"* confronting the prosperous king about his adulterous affair with another man's wife. Nathan spoke truth, as prophets must, and Israel's greatest king confessed his heartless sin to God. This was not the first time Nathan sowed God's truth into David's soul; there had been another such moment, arguably a larger one.

Settled into his newly built palace, David contemplated the irony: "Here I am, living in a house of cedar, while the ark of God remains in a tent."[221] His yen to build a more suitable structure for God's presence was, in a way, commendable, but it was just that: David's idea, not God's. Uncharacteristically, Nathan replied without consulting God, "Whatever you have in mind, go ahead and do it, for the LORD is with you,"[222] he said to the king. There they were—Israel's leaders presuming to know and pursue what they thought best for God without seeking His will. But "people's lives are not their own; it is not for them to

---

[220] 2 Samuel 12:7 KJV
[221] 2 Samuel 7:2
[222] 2 Samuel 7:3

direct their steps."[223] God said to Nathan later that night, "Go and tell my servant David, 'This is what the LORD says: Are you the one to build me a house to dwell in?'"[224] It was neither the king's place nor within his capability to decide what was best for God, whose plans had been established from before the creation of the world. Instead, God sent Nathan back to David bearing *His* covenantal plan—that the Messiah would come through the king's lineage: "Your house and your kingdom will endure forever before me; your throne will be established forever."[225] David listened in humility and responded in submission, "Who am I, Sovereign LORD, and what is my family, that you have brought me this far?"[226] adding, "Do as you promised, so that your name will be great forever."[227]

Even God's people can speak hastily without first seeking Him, so we do well to listen with discernment for God's voice. For our God is the God of grace, and with words of strength, wisdom, and truth He still speaks to and through those who hear Him, aligning us with His plans, purposes, and will. We who live in Christ by faith are united in Him, and it delights God to work through each of us for the growth of all of us. So with submitted, discerning, and loving hearts, let us speak truth, as Nathan did.

---

[223] Jeremiah 10:23
[224] 2 Samuel 7:5
[225] 2 Samuel 7:16
[226] 2 Samuel 7:18
[227] 2 Samuel 7:25–26

David

"Guide me in Your truth and teach me, for You are God my Savior, and my hope is in You all day long."[228] *Amen.*

---

[228] Psalm 25:5

David Spoke Faith

N o one names their child Goliath, do they? I didn't think so. The name has been used plenty throughout the millennia, but only as metaphor for seemingly insurmountable opposition. Sports always has its Goliaths, the perennial powerhouses that dominate year-in and year-out, and we apply the tag to "the system" and its matrixed components—politicians, corporations, and influential individuals. But no one names their child Goliath, for the Philistine specimen was both an overconfident bully and an underachieving loser. He was intimidating in appearance: larger than any professional wrestler, and strong; he wore 125 pounds of armor, and the mere tip of his spear weighed 15 pounds, roughly as much as the steel ball used in shot put competition. "Whenever the Israelites saw the man, they all fled from him in great fear."[229] Veni, vidi, vamoose. (I came, I saw, I ran the other way.)

David saw things differently. A veritable colossus stood before him—there was no doubt about that. But the battle against him was not David's; it belonged to the One who, though unseen, was infinitely stronger than any Goliath His people could ever face. "You come against me with sword and spear and javelin," said David, "but I come against you in the name of the LORD Almighty, the God of the armies of Israel, whom you have defied. This day the LORD will deliver you into

---

[229] 1 Samuel 17:24

my hands ... and the whole world will know that there is a God in Israel."[230] His were the words of faith—"confidence in what we hope for and assurance about what we do not see."[231] Then with one stone skillfully hurled from a shepherd's sling, Israel's menace was no more!

Not all Goliaths are external; many challenge us from within. Fear and pride in all their manifestations rise up against us in overwhelming proportions, and in such times we must fortify our soul with words of faith. When despair advanced against David, for instance, he strengthened himself with hope, "Why are you cast down, O my soul, and why are you in turmoil within me? Hope in God; for I shall again praise him, my salvation and my God."[232] Feeling alone amid conspiracy, the king assured himself of God's faithfulness: "For God alone, O my soul, wait in silence, for my hope is from him. He only is my rock and my salvation, my fortress; I shall not be shaken."[233] Recalling God's goodness from the past gave David peace of mind in the present—"Return, O my soul, to your rest; for the LORD has dealt bountifully with you."[234]

Paul reminded the Corinthian believers, "it is written: 'I believed; therefore I have spoken.' Since we have that same

---

[230] 1 Samuel 17:45–46
[231] Hebrews 11:1
[232] Psalm 42:5 ESV
[233] Psalm 62:5–6 ESV
[234] Psalm 116:7 ESV

Spirit of faith, we also believe and therefore speak."[235] May this be our way of life, as well—may we speak faith, as David did.

Father, I believe. Grace me to speak Your greatness in the freedom and joy of faith. In Christ I pray. Amen.

---

[235] 2 Corinthians 4:13

Section Ten

The Gerasene Demoniac

"**T**he reason the Son of God appeared was to destroy the devil's work,"[236] declared John to the early church. It was a primary purpose for Jesus, one He ultimately completed in His atoning sacrifice and His resurrection victory over death. Yet Jesus' power and authority were also amply evident throughout His earthly ministry, as Peter recalled to Cornelius and those gathered in his home: "You know what has happened throughout the province of Judea ... how God anointed Jesus of Nazareth with the Holy Spirit and power, and how he went around doing good and healing all who were under the power of the devil, because God was with him."[237] One such beneficiary of Jesus' work was a man from Gerasa, a small village in the Decapolis, or "ten cities," a region east of the Sea of Galilee. Jesus found him possessed by many demons—driven to harm himself, unable to control himself, and living in tombs and

---

[236] 1 John 3:8
[237] Acts 10:37–38

117

caves. By the time Jesus departed mere hours later, the man was "sitting there, dressed and in his right mind."[238]

Thankfully, not many of us have ever been possessed by a demon and driven to such horrific extremes; in fact, to us the man's plight may seem unrelatable. Yet the apostle Paul reminds us we, too, once "followed the ways of this world and of the ruler of the kingdom of the air."[239] In this sense, the Gerasene's story is our story; it is the story of the gospel, "the power of God that brings salvation to everyone who believes."[240] As this man was delivered from the evil one, so too have all who live in Christ by faith; by God's grace what we were is not who we are. We can relate to the psalmist and confess with him: "When my heart was grieved and my spirit embittered, I was senseless and ignorant; I was a brute beast before you. Yet I am always with you; you hold me by my right hand. You guide me with your counsel, and afterward you will take me into glory."[241]

Discussion of spiritual forces of evil can be unnerving, so we begin with the end in mind: Jesus lives in us, and Jesus always wins. Consider the man from Gerasa, for in the love of Christ and by His power and authority, the former demoniac became free. Watch and see.

---

[238] Mark 5:15

[239] Ephesians 2:2

[240] Romans 1:16

[241] Psalm 73:21–24

Spoiler Alert: We Win

I believe it was in the fifth grade when a close friend turned against me, and with him several others. As I walked home one day not long after, they launched a steady barrage of snowballs at me, relentlessly reloading from northern Michigan's endless supply of winter white. It so happened, though, that at the point of ambush was someone shoveling his driveway. He wore a varsity jacket, so he was likely a high school junior or senior, and because he was in the line of fire, he joined me. So together we battled a small detachment of preadolescents—I lobbing lazy, high-arching "air cover" and the big guy firing frozen spheres arrow-straight, at high speed, and with great precision. It was enough: the enemy scattered, and I walked safely home. "We" had won.

We don't know *how* the man from Gerasa obtained an "impure spirit" or *how* he had become possessed by a "legion" of demons; we only know that he suffered greatly under the oppressive powers of darkness. Constantly tormented in body, mind, and soul, he had become a frighteningly "fierce"[242] man of unrestrainable strength, "always crying out and cutting himself with stones."[243] But authority understands authority, and when the demons in him saw Jesus arriving, they in self-interest drove their helpless host into His presence: the man "ran

---

[242] Matthew 8:28 ESV
[243] Mark 5:5 ESV

and fell on his knees in front of him."[244] Then at the top of the man's voice, they collectively shouted at Jesus, "What do you want with me, Jesus, Son of the Most High God? In God's name don't torture me!"[245] (Ironic, isn't it—bullies begging for mercy in the face of defeat?) At Jesus' command, the demons scattered, and the man was safe. "He" had won.

Our "walk home" is filled with battles, for we "struggle ... against the powers of this dark world and against the spiritual forces of evil."[246] Yet as painful and difficult as these times are, in Jesus we have already won. The Father "has rescued us from the dominion of darkness and brought us into the kingdom of the Son he loves."[247] No matter how tortured our past or how hopeless things appear, we have won. No matter who is against us or how great their number, we have won. Though our foes might attack us or our friends flee our side, we have won. Then in the confidence of Christ and in His power, we face our enemies; be they addictions, frustrations, rejections, or regrets, we can face them, knowing this: we are in Christ, and Jesus always wins.

The one who is in you is greater than the one who is in the world. (1 John 4:4)

---

[244] Mark 5:6
[245] Mark 5:7
[246] Ephesians 6:12
[247] Colossians 1:13

Father, thank You for this assurance: Jesus has defeated our enemy, and in Christ I have, too. You are God, and I am safe. Help me always to remember this and to rest in You. In Christ I pray. Amen.

What We Were Is Not Who We Are

If there is a greater personal transformation in fiction than that of Ebenezer Scrooge, it does not readily come to mind. For over 150 years, Charles Dickens' miserly protagonist has served as a metaphor for callousness and greed, but his story is really one of conviction and change—his spiritual awakening, the realization of wrong, a plea for mercy, and a newborn compassion for others. His testimony is that of one made new, changed from the inside out. "And it was always said of him, that he knew how to keep Christmas well, if any man alive possessed the knowledge."[248] So why do we still tether the old money lender to his former "Humbug" existence? Why also do we do the same in real life, defining, for instance, both the Samaritan woman and Mary Magdalene by who they were *before* they encountered Jesus? Did Jesus *leave* them that way? Of course not, nor will the man from Gerasa—the one "sitting there, dressed and in his right mind"[249]—ever be a demoniac again.

Writing to believers in Ephesus, Paul recalled their life without Christ, when they, like all of us, "followed the ways of this world and of the ruler of the kingdom of the air, the spirit who is now at work in those who are disobedient ... gratifying the cravings of our flesh and following its desires and

---

[248] Charles Dickens, *A Christmas Carol*, Enriched Classic (New York: Pocket Books, 2007), 104.
[249] Mark 5:15

thoughts."[250] What sorts of people were we who now make up the church? Paul's list of sins reads like a rap sheet: "sexually immoral ... idolaters ... thieves ... the greedy ... slanderers," he reminded his Corinthian readers, adding, "And that is what some of you were."[251] Did you catch his hidden proclamation of freedom? *"Were"* — the past tense indicating the former identity of a bygone life. For Jesus has not defined us by our sin, *nor should we*. "But you were washed," Paul continued, "you were sanctified, you were justified in the name of the Lord Jesus Christ and by the Spirit of our God."[252]

Behind us lay our shackles of shame, for though we still sin, our sin is not who we are any more, nor will it ever be again.

Made new in Christ, we are "called to live in freedom ... [and to] use [our] freedom to serve one another in love."[253] Behind us lay our shackles of shame, for though we still sin, our sin is not who we are any more, nor will it ever be again. God knows this, our enemy knows this, and we must know it, too, so that we run and thrive in newness of life. For we have been united with the sinless Christ—He lives in us, and we in Him—and Jesus always wins.

---

[250] Ephesians 2:2–3
[251] 1 Corinthians 6:9–11
[252] 1 Corinthians 6:11
[253] Galatians 5:13 NLT

You were once darkness, but now you are light in the Lord. Live as children of light. (Ephesians 5:8).

Father, send us Your Spirit that we would better know the truth and riches of who we are in Christ, and that, enlightened this way, we would live daily in His power and always for His glory. Amen.

Resistance Training

In my senior year in high school, we chose *Charlie's Aunt* for our class play, and I assumed the role of Sir Francis Chesney. Between two of my scenes lay a sizable gap, so each night during this interlude another production member and I would slip away from practice to access the school's weight room. Over the six weeks or so before our debut, I increased my bench press maximum by forty-five pounds. Resistance training did not make me a better actor, but it made me stronger.

As people in Christ, we are called to resist—to exert ourselves against the weight of spiritual oppression. His enemy is our enemy; we struggle not against physical or ideological combatants, but "against the powers of this dark world and against the spiritual forces of evil in the heavenly realms,"[254] those that rise up in rebellion against God. Our battle is real, but how do we detect attacks from a silent foe we cannot see? We discern his voice of falsehood in opposition to truth—his attempts to deceive us into questioning God's Word or disbelieving it entirely. He tempts us to think of God as less than He is, and he entices us to sate our "evil desire,"[255] which leads to sin and death. All of this he does through lies.

How then do we fight this invisible battle? We stand—we are called to stand. "Put on the full armor of God, so that when the day of evil comes, you may be able to *stand your ground*,

---

[254] Ephesians 6:12
[255] James 1:14

and after you have done everything, *to stand*,"[256] Paul writes. We plant ourselves squarely on who the Bible says God is and who God says we are in Christ Jesus. Discerning truth, we "take captive every thought to make it obedient to Christ."[257] We "offer [ourselves] to God as those who have been brought from death to life, and [we] offer every part of [ourselves] to him as an instrument of righteousness."[258] We remain "alert and of sober mind [for our] enemy the devil prowls about like a roaring lion looking for someone to devour."[259] We "*resist* him, *standing firm* in the faith,"[260] knowing this promise from James: "Resist the devil, and he will flee from you."[261] Then "the God of all grace ... will himself restore [us] and make [us] strong, firm and steadfast."[262] We will emerge from the trial of temptation, changed—strengthened and made confident in victory—for we stand in Christ, and Jesus always wins.

Away from me, Satan! (Matthew 4:10)

Father, temptations lure us, and we are easily deceived. Send us Your Spirit to remind us what is true and to strengthen

---

[256] Ephesians 6:13, emphasis added
[257] 2 Corinthians 10:5
[258] Romans 6:13
[259] 1 Peter 5:8
[260] 1 Peter 5:9, emphasis added
[261] James 4:7
[262] 1 Peter 5:10

us against him who is false. Thank You that, against deception and temptation, we need only to stand in Christ. Amen.

A Life of Meaning

I sn't it amazing that our God of limitless power is also our God of infinite love? Think about it for a minute: if God were all-powerful but imperfect in love, we might live our days in fear of caprice; but without indomitable power, on the other hand, a God of flawless love would be constrained in His ability to express it. Praise God, He is perfect in both! This then is the Gerasene's story: in great love, Jesus cared for a man abandoned to a tortured existence, and in unmatched authority, He dispersed his quaking tormentors of darkness. The man had become free—*free from* demonic authority, and *free to* follow Jesus.

As his deliverer got in the boat to leave, the grateful man "begged to go with him."[263] Who could blame him? Yet Jesus had in mind something even greater for him—the gift of impact, or what we might call "making a difference." "Go home to your own people and tell them how much the Lord has done for you, and how he has had mercy on you,"[264] He replied. So equipped with the one thing he needed for success, the true story of Jesus' work in his life, "the man went away and began to tell in the Decapolis how much Jesus had done for him. And all the people were amazed."[265] How many were "rescued ... from the dominion of darkness and brought ... into the kingdom of the

---

[263] Mark 5:18
[264] Mark 5:19
[265] Mark 5:20

Son"[266] because of one man's testimony, we cannot say. But we do know that when Jesus returned to the area of the Decapolis and was asked to heal a man there, He "took him aside, *away from the crowd.*"[267] In a region where He had once been asked to leave, a crowd now gathered to see Him—perhaps the fruit of a one-time demoniac turned faithful witness.

Not many of us have had to suffer the way this man did, but we have been rescued from darkness through the power and love of Christ, which is to say we have a story to tell. We do not need to defend our testimony, because it is true. We do not have to go about changing people, because we cannot. We need only to witness—to tell what we have seen—knowing people will be encouraged and God will be glorified. Could there be a more meaningful life than to make a kingdom impact for eternity? By God's grace we can, for we are in Christ, and by now we know this to be true. Jesus. Always. Wins.

Well done, good and faithful servant!
(Matthew 25:21)

Father, You have graced us with Your favor and given us a story. Grace us again with the opportunity and courage to share it. Bear fruit for Your kingdom through us, Your people. Be glorified. In Jesus' name we pray. Amen.

---

[266] Colossians 1:13
[267] Mark 7:33, emphasis added

Section Eleven

Paul

W riting to his young protégé Timothy, an aging apostle proclaimed, "Christ Jesus came into the world to save sinners," adding poignantly, "of whom I am the worst."[268] "I was shown mercy," Paul continued, "so that in me, the worst of sinners, Christ Jesus might display his immense patience as an example for those who would believe in him and receive eternal life."[269] Thirty years or so earlier, he would have confessed neither Christ as Lord nor himself a sinner. The former Pharisee had changed.

Paul was brilliant. As a young man under the tutelage of Gamaliel—one of the great minds of that time—Paul was, he would later recall, "advancing in Judaism beyond many of my own age among my people."[270] Even Festus, the governor of

---

[268] 1 Timothy 1:15
[269] 1 Timothy 1:16
[270] Galatians 1:14

Judea, knew of the apostle's reputation for "great learning."[271] So, too, Paul was driven, "extremely zealous for the traditions of my fathers,"[272] in his words, faultless as to legalistic righteousness and relentless in the persecution of Christians who celebrated a righteousness apart from the law. He was a force, and he had a future—but not the one he had anticipated.

Paul's encounter with Jesus on the road to Damascus is well known. Knocked to the ground in a flash of blinding light, Paul was chosen and called by the risen Christ. "I am Jesus, whom you are persecuting," the Lord said, "Now get up and stand on your feet. I have appeared to you to appoint you as a servant and as a witness of what you have seen and will see of me."[273] "Though I was once a blasphemer and a persecutor and a violent man," Paul would testify long afterward, "I was shown mercy because I acted in ignorance and unbelief."[274] His gifted mind would of necessity be renewed, not unto "ignorance" this time but in truth: "I did not receive [the gospel] from any man," he said, "nor was I taught it; rather, I received it by revelation from Jesus Christ."[275]

The reborn Paul was still brilliant but now also understanding; he was still zealous yet now fruitful as well. The believers who once lived in fear of him marveled at him: "The

---

[271] Acts 26:24
[272] Galatians 1:14
[273] Acts 26:15–16
[274] 1 Timothy 1:13
[275] Galatians 1:12

man who formerly persecuted us is now preaching the faith he once tried to destroy."[276] He had changed inwardly, which glorified God outwardly. Watch and see.

---

[276] Galatians 1:23

Realigning Our Thoughts

R esponding to a middle-school "Bible challenge," my wife Peggy had established a daily pattern of reading one chapter per day from God's Word. The more she learned about God, the more she wanted to know about Him. By the time she reached her mid-teens, Peggy knew she believed in God and in Jesus Christ, His Son, so she began to wonder, "If this is all true, what must God want from me?" While reading a short summary of the gospel one day, she came to realize, "What God wants from me, is *me*." Peggy was right—discovering Jesus demands a response, as the apostle Paul likewise found. Fallen to the ground in a brilliant flash of heavenly light, the ruthless Pharisee somehow mustered the two most vital questions one can ask: "Who are you, Lord?"[277] and "What shall I do, Lord?"[278]

To discover Christ is to reach the realization that God is true, His character flawless, and His ways unsearchably wise. It is also a rendezvous with the humbling truth that our natural way of thinking is hostile to God and unable to submit to Him. Our actions follow our hearts and minds, so there must be for us a

> *Our actions follow our hearts and minds, so there must be for us a new direction with a lifetime of next steps.*

---

[277] Acts 22:8
[278] Acts 22:10

new direction with a lifetime of next steps. Indeed, there is: *we align our minds with where we are going*. Paul instructed us: "Since, then, you have been raised with Christ, set your hearts on things above, where Christ is, seated at the right hand of God. Set your minds on things above, not on earthly things."[279] What might this look like? Paul gives us a glimpse: "Whatever is true, whatever is noble, whatever is right, whatever is pure, whatever is lovely, whatever is admirable—if anything is excellent or praiseworthy—think about such things."[280]

Then is "right thinking" some kind of new law to pursue in our own power, one more rule to remember and manage? Hardly. God has given us a new way—a relational way—of life. It is the way of God's Spirit in us. Paul assured the early church: "You are not controlled by your sinful nature. You are controlled by the Spirit if you have the Spirit of God living in you."[281] He said, "Those who live in accordance with the Spirit have their minds set on what the Spirit desires," and "... the mind governed by the Spirit is life and peace."[282] We live in daily relationship with God, "be[ing] transformed by the renewing of [our] mind."[283] So today, we listen for His voice, trust in His promises, align our thinking with His truth, and go forward in His power to do what He has prepared for us to do.

---

[279] Colossians 3:1–2
[280] Philippians 4:8
[281] Romans 8:9 NLT
[282] Romans 8:5–6
[283] Romans 12:2

*Do not conform to the pattern of this world, but
be transformed by the renewing of your mind.
Then you will be able to test and approve what
God's will is—his good, pleasing and perfect
will. (Romans 12:2)*

*Father, You are wise, and Your ways are so recognizably
different than my own. Send Your Spirit to lead me, that I would
set my heart and mind on You and do what You call me to do
today. In Christ I pray. Amen.*

Remembering Our Call

B ecause we valued input from local marketplace perspectives, our leadership team convened a group of independent insurance agents who sold our company's products in their respective cities and towns. When the conversation tangentially alluded to the regulatory climate in a neighboring state, one of the sales professionals quipped, "In [that state], a crooked politician is one who won't *stay* bought!" We all had a good guffaw at the easy target of "politics as usual," yet the story is reminiscent of a deeper purpose for us who have found full and forever life in Christ—our call to *stay free.*

The young Galatian church had found themselves infiltrated and influenced by those who insisted on pursuing God's favor through legalistic means, and it showed. "Where is that joyful and grateful spirit you felt?"[284] Paul asked of their fleeting joy. "After starting your new lives in the Spirit, why are you now trying to become perfect by your own human effort?"[285] Now, if anyone understood the end result of human effort, it was Paul, "a Pharisee, descended from Pharisees"[286] and "extremely zealous for the traditions of [his] fathers."[287] "As for righteousness," he once recalled, "I obeyed the law without fault."[288]

---

[284] Galatians 4:15 NLT
[285] Galatians 3:3 NLT
[286] Acts 23:6
[287] Galatians 1:14
[288] Philippians 3:6 NLT

Then what did human accomplishments and worldly accolades gain for the apostle? "I consider everything a loss," he wrote, "because of the surpassing worth of knowing Christ Jesus my Lord, for whose sake I have lost all things. I consider them garbage, that I may gain Christ and be found in him, not having a righteousness of my own that comes from the law, but that which is through faith in Christ—the righteousness that comes from God on the basis of faith."[289] Paul had sought God's favor through the merit of his own perfection, only to find it through the grace and perfection of Christ. There was no comparison, and there was no going back.

"Christ has truly set us free. Now make sure that you *stay* free, and don't get tied up again in slavery to the law."[290] Paul's words speak as much to us as to the Galatians, so how do we remain in spiritual freedom, and where do we regain "that joyful and grateful spirit"? Personally, whenever I find myself in despair, doubt, anxiousness and the like, I have found the best thing to do is to savor what is true and remember that in His initiating love God called us to Himself—boldly and by name. "And having called [us],"

> *Paul had sought God's favor through the merit of his own perfection, only to find it through the grace and perfection of Christ.*

---

[289] Philippians 3:8–9
[290] Galatians 5:1 NLT, emphasis added

Paul assures us that God "gave [us] right standing with himself … he gave [us] his glory."[291] In Christ, we have God's favor, and we are free from the impossible task of earning it. May we then *stay* free and, in the confidence of liberty, serve.

> *You, my brothers and sisters, were called to be free. (Galatians 5:13)*

Father, though I know I cannot earn Your acceptance, I am still tempted to try. Remind me of Your boundless love for me, that I would look upon You with confidence and reach out to others in freedom, gratitude, and joy. In Christ I pray. Amen.

---

[291] Romans 8:30 NLT

Rethinking Our Suffering

"Join with me in suffering, like a good soldier of Christ Jesus."[292] *Paul, to Timothy*

N ow come the veterans. The parade has delighted us with bands playing, horses clopping, notables waving, and candy strewn to scampering children. And now come the veterans of war. We smile, wave, cheer, and salute, all to honor those who battled to protect our freedoms. Yet our appreciation of liberty is faint compared to theirs, for who can identify with freedom as much as those who have risked everything, sacrificed dearly, and grieved deeply to preserve it? What words could they possibly speak to convey an understanding only they can know?

Though all the apostles endured persecution for proclaiming Christ as Lord, Paul's life was especially characterized by it. He was imprisoned more often, flogged more severely, exposed to death more repeatedly, thrice beaten with rods, and shipwrecked three times as well; the list goes on. We naturally recoil at his extreme afflictions, quietly questioning, perhaps, our resolve to endure the same, yet in his suffering for Jesus Paul grew to understand Him more deeply, trust Him more completely, and rejoice in Him more fully. "I *delight* in weaknesses, in insults, in hardships, in persecutions, in difficulties," reflected the battle-tested veteran, "For when I am weak, then

---

[292] 2 Timothy 2:3

140

I am strong."[293] Recalling a time when he and his companions found themselves "under great pressure, far beyond our ability to endure,"[294] Paul ultimately realized "this happened that we might not rely on ourselves but on God."[295] He had grown to "glory in [his] sufferings, because ... suffering produces perseverance ... character ... and hope"[296] in God whose "love has been poured out into our hearts through the Holy Spirit."[297]

Many believers have experienced at least some degree of rejection or ridicule for their faith in Christ, and in some parts of the world they endure terrible persecution. As we consider our journey, though, wouldn't you agree it is not marginalization or ostracism for the sake of Christ we regret, rather the times we suppressed our faith to avoid it? We cannot "do-over" the weaker moments of our past, but we can let them remind us that the sting of opportunities lost pains us far more than any cost of opportunities seized. Peter wrote: "It is better, *if it is God's will*, to suffer for doing good than for doing evil";[298] moreover, in these times, we identify more closely with Christ Jesus who endured rejection and wrath for us. So "if you suffer as a Christian, do not be ashamed, but praise God that you bear that name."[299] "For our light and momentary troubles are

---

[293] 2 Corinthians 12:10, emphasis added
[294] 2 Corinthians 1:8
[295] 2 Corinthians 1:9
[296] Romans 5:3–4
[297] Romans 5:5
[298] 1 Peter 3:17, emphasis added
[299] 1 Peter 4:16

achieving for us an eternal glory that far outweighs them all."[300] Amen. Come, Lord Jesus.

Father, however You call me today to share the gospel of Your Son or to serve in His name, send Your Spirit to lead me. If ever I must suffer for doing good, sustain me with joy. Amen.

---

[300] 2 Corinthians 4:17

Retaining Our Focus

My niece Meghan was an outstanding middle-distance track athlete in high school, frequently winning her events. At the team's annual awards banquet her sophomore year, the coach said of her, "Meghan learned to run through pain," a quality often distinguishing the best from the rest. She had grown in grit, exchanging comfort for excellence; she had matured as a runner and become a winner. Perseverance has a transforming effect all its own, and Meghan was named the "most improved" member of the team that season.

It was James, the Lord's brother, who wrote: "Consider it pure joy, my brothers and sisters, whenever you face trials of many kinds, because you know that the testing of your faith produces perseverance."[301] We know from Paul the test of physical persecution, of course, yet our trials also include the worldly enticements that distract us and the devilish deceptions that discourage us from growing in kingdom effectiveness. Jesus taught, for instance, that when we let "life's worries, riches and pleasures"[302] choke us like weeds, we remain immature and unfruitful. He said, also, we can expect people to insult, persecute, and falsely say all kinds of evil against us because of Him.[303] These are meant to intimidate us, yet in reality they are but hindrances and entanglements we are called to "throw off"

---

[301] James 1:2–3
[302] Luke 8:14
[303] Matthew 5:11

as we "run with perseverance the race mapped out for us."[304] For we run not just to reach a finish line—there is impactful work for us along the way. Indeed, Jesus said that by persevering, those who hear the word and retain it "produce a crop."[305] Paul summarized a life of purposeful pursuit this way: "I consider my life worth nothing to me; my only aim is to *finish the race and complete the task* the Lord Jesus has given me—the task of testifying to the good news of God's grace."[306]

Then we run with focus, "fixing our eyes on Jesus, the pioneer and perfecter of faith,"[307] and we "consider him who endured such opposition from sinners so that [we] will not grow weary and lose heart."[308] "Forgetting what is behind and straining toward what is ahead," we, like Paul, "press on toward the goal to win the prize for which God has called [us] heavenward in Christ Jesus."[309] So, we focus—"we fix our eyes not on what is seen, but on what is unseen, since what is seen is temporary, but what is unseen is eternal."[310] We mature as runners; we become winners.

Let perseverance finish its work so that you may
be mature and complete, not lacking anything.
(James 1:4)

---

[304] Hebrews 12:1
[305] Luke 8:15
[306] Acts 20:24, emphasis added
[307] Hebrews 12:2
[308] Hebrews 12:3
[309] Philippians 3:13–14
[310] 2 Corinthians 4:18

Paul

Father, lead us in the course You have mapped out for us today. Strengthen us to throw off all that would hinder and entangle us. Grace us to fix our eyes on You and to run well in Christ. Amen.

Section Twelve

John

Partnered in the fishing business with his brother James—and they together with Peter and Andrew of Bethsaida—John, like the others, was obviously "unschooled [and] ordinary."[311] He had his rough edges and they showed; for example, when the Samaritans rejected Jesus, he and James asked: "Lord, do you want us to call fire down from heaven to destroy them?"[312] In fact, Jesus had a nickname for the brothers to share—Boanerges, which means "sons of thunder."[313] Then there was the time when they, together with their mother, pulled Jesus aside and lobbied for personal seat licenses on either side of the King's eternal throne.[314] (How gauche!)

There were certain events during Jesus' ministry that He shared only with Peter, James, and John, including His

---

[311] Acts 4:13
[312] Luke 9:54
[313] Mark 3:17
[314] Matthew 20:20–21

147

transfiguration and His anguish in Gethsemane. After the ascension, John seems to have been paired with Peter more than the others, for instance at the healing of the lame man and the aftermath of persecution,[315] as well as their joint encounter with Simon the sorcerer.[316] John was Peter's opposite, a contrast that illumines all the more John's quieter, more contemplative persona. He was seemingly more able to express affection—it was he who laid his head against Jesus' chest at their last meal in the upper room—and sensitive toward that received from others. In three short years, this "son of thunder" had come humbly to see himself as "the disciple Jesus loved."[317]

Paul once wrote that, though all else pass away, three things remain forever—faith, hope, and love. As John outlived the other eleven disciples, he matured in faith and grew in love well into his nineties. He wrote prolifically about love—the love shared between the Father and the Son, the love of God for the world, and the love of believers for others. "If we love one another," he assured us, "God lives in us and his love is made complete in us."[318] We will be transformed. Watch and see.

---

[315] Acts 3:1-4:31
[316] Acts 8:14-24
[317] See John 13:23; 19:26; 20:2; 21:7; and 21:20.
[318] 1 John 4:12

Resting in God's Personal Love

"My life changed when I realized Jesus really loves me," recalled a friend. I drew a short quick breath, startled not at what he said but because he was the third person in the short span of one year to say this same thing verbatim. All three had been believers for quite some time beforehand—trusting in Christ alone for salvation and grateful for it—yet each had arrived at an epiphany in life when their eyes opened, barriers fell, love flowed, and life changed. Their stories resonated with me, for my life, too, had changed when I realized Jesus really loves me. I had begun a daily pattern of reading God's Word, then writing down what it was saying to me, how it was affecting me, and in turn my prayerful response. Soon I began to sense more deeply both God's immeasurable love for all of humankind and His personal love for me. The palpable presence of His Spirit opened my heart to joy, and over time I have found myself criticizing less and caring more, stressing less and resting more, doubting less and trusting more. He was doing through His love what I could not do by my will—He was changing me. Thankfully, He still is; it's a process.

Of all the disciples, it was John who understood—or at least expressed—most deeply the intimacy of Jesus' personal love. Five times in his gospel account, this former fisherman identified himself as "the disciple whom Jesus loved."[319] This was

---

[319] See John 13:23; 19:26; 20:2; 21:7; and 21:20.

not to suggest the Messiah loved him more than the others—all of the disciples rightly could have said the same about themselves, and perhaps each of them did. Rather, John's confession was a matter of identity, as if to confess, "my worth is complete in this, and only this: Jesus loves me." John savored this wonder; he embraced it and expressed it over and over again as if to process the unfathomable. Jesus really loved him, and his life had changed.

Jesus once urged His disciples, "Come with me by yourselves to a quiet place and get some rest,"[320] and indeed sometimes the most vital next step for us in life is

Sometimes the most vital next step for us in life is to stop for a time and rest in His love for us.

to stop for a time and rest in His love for us. Perhaps for you today this means reminiscing on specific things He has done for you—and in you—in the past. Maybe it is going on a walk with God, speaking openly and listening quietly to Him who calls us His friends. Priority time in the Word of God is reliably transformational, for through the Word of God the Spirit of God speaks the truth of His love into our longing soul. As He leads, sit with this for a while, contemplate God's love for you, and take it personally. He really loves you.

---

[320] Mark 6:31

John

We love because he first loved us.
(1 John 4:19 ESV)

Father, Your Word says, "Be still, and know that I am
God."[321] Calm me, that I would be still before You and know
Your love for me. I give thanks to You, for You are good, and
Your love endures forever. In Christ I pray. Amen.

---

[321] Psalm 46:10

151

Living in God's Eternal Love

Thomas had voiced the question the other disciples were likely pondering—*How could they know the way to where Jesus was going?*—and Jesus' answer had been profound. Now it was Philip's turn to speak up: "Lord, show us the Father and that will be enough for us."[322] It had to be a frustration for Jesus on the eve of His crucifixion—He had covered this ground with them before—but at the heart of the matter was life itself, so Jesus taught them. "Don't you know me, Philip, even after I have been among you such a long time? Anyone who has seen me has seen the Father. How can you say, 'Show us the Father'? Don't you believe that I am in the Father, and that the Father is in me? … Believe me when I say that I am in the Father and the Father is in me."[323] We can sympathize with Philip, for the existence of the Father and the Son as one, each living in the other, is an enigma for finite minds to fathom and a deeper intimacy than timid hearts will dare to brave. Yet this is who God is, and it is this unifying relationship into which He calls us, having paid the ultimate price to do so. Looking ahead to His resurrection, Jesus continued, "On that day you will realize that *I am in my Father*, and *you are in me*, and *I am in you*."[324]

This is difficult for us to imagine, but it is true—"All who declare that Jesus is the Son of God have *God living in them,*

---

[322] John 14:8
[323] John 14:9-11
[324] John 14:20, emphasis added

and they live in God."[325] Then as "God is love,"[326] we can love as He does, for "love comes from God."[327] This is pure love, the patient and kind sort of love that keeps no record of wrongs and rejoices with the truth—always protecting, trusting, hoping, and persevering.[328] It is liberating love, so complete and secure that we can "love [our] enemies and pray for those who perse-cute [us]."[329] Yet God's love is also the gauge by which we know our incomplete notion of love falls short. We are tempted, then, to con-demn ourselves and with-draw from God in shame or to make love a rule for us to keep in order to gain His favor. God does not condemn us, however, nor should we. And true love is not our means of reaching up to God to earn His favor; rather it is proof that He has reached out to us to show us His grace. Then, "as we live in God, our love grows more perfect. So we will not be afraid on the day of judgment, but we can face him with confidence because we live like Jesus

> *True love is not our means of reaching up to God to earn His favor; rather it is proof that He has reached out to us to show us His grace.*

---

[325] 1 John 4:15 NLT, emphasis added
[326] 1 John 4:8 NLT
[327] 1 John 4:7 NLT
[328] 1 Corinthians 13:4-8
[329] Matthew 5:44

here in this world."[330] This is His doing in us; this is our joy in Him.

> *God is love. Whoever lives in love lives in God,*
> *and God in them. (1 John 4:16)*

Father, we pray Your love will grow more abundantly in us and flow more fruitfully from us to those we encounter today. Such freedom! Such joy! Thank You. In Jesus' name we pray. Amen.

---

[330] 1 John 4:17 NLT

Serving in God's Relational Love

W hy is it that the best we ever feel is when God works through us to assist another in need of help? Personally, no monetary compensation has ever offered more lasting and fulfilling joy than being a blessing to someone in some way. Strange, isn't it? But then, maybe we shouldn't be surprised, for Jesus said, "If you keep my commands, you will remain in my love, just as I have kept my Father's commands and remain in his love. I have told you this so that *my joy may be in you and that your joy may be complete.* My command is this: Love each other as I have loved you."[331]

This Biblical love of which Jesus speaks is active love. It elicits warm feelings and noble thoughts, certainly, yet it stirs also in the deeper chambers of our soul, awakening the servant within from slumber. This love does not chafe at personal inconvenience, nor does it shrink from the enormity of its call. God's love never stops at obstacles; it moves mountains—it loves anyway. And in love, God grows us even through failures too numerous to count. Here, then, are a few lessons learned along the way.

> *God's love never stops at obstacles; it moves mountains—it loves anyway.*

Follow Jesus' lead. Jesus did "only what he [saw] his Father doing"[332]

---

[331] John 15:10–12, emphasis added
[332] John 5:19

and said "just what the Father ... told [him] to say."[333] We are likewise called to speak and act only as His Spirit leads us, for we are "created in Christ Jesus to do good works, *which God prepared in advance for us to do*."[334]

Join in. For years, I sensed a call to share God's love with the incarcerated, but it was only when a friend invited me to serve on a prison ministry team that I actually engaged. If you sense the Spirit urging you to minister in some way but you don't know how, join someone already doing what you are being called to do.

Use your gift. The Spirit gifts us "just as He determines,"[335] so each of us has a role amid all of us. Whatever your gift may be—helping, teaching, administration, intercession, leadership, hospitality, or anything else—act in it. Then listen to the symphony of the Spirit's wind flowing through an entire orchestra of individual instruments, that is the church.

Seize the day. Life presents its momentous occasions along the way, but it chiefly comes at us in daily doses of small measures. The call to act in love also comes in ways unexpected and easily overlooked. God has prepared these for you—and you for these—so watch for them, and step into them as they unfold before you.

Do it anyway. If others discourage you from God's call to sacrificial service or if Satan entices you elsewhere or if you

---

[333] John 12:50
[334] Ephesians 2:10, emphasis added
[335] 1 Corinthians 12:11

simply don't feel like being selfless, engage anyway and serve as you are being called to serve. There will be fruit.

✓ *Embrace God's favor.* Before you do anything in Jesus' name, remember that His love for you is infinite. Serve then not to gain God's favor, but in the joy and humility that you already have it.

> *Beloved, if God so loved us, we also ought to love one another. (1 John 4:11 ESV)*

Father, You have poured out Your love and grace upon us. Show us and lead us in what You are calling us to say and do today. Be glorified in us, Your people in Christ Jesus. Amen.

Maturing in God's Transformational Love

> *Dear friends, now we are children of God, and*
> *what we will be has not yet been made known.*
> *But we know that when Christ appears, we*
> *shall be like him, for we shall see him as he is.*
> *(1 John 3:2)*

Peggy and I find yard work to be relaxing and gratifying, and of the two of us it is usually she who has the clearer mental picture of a well-tended garden. It helps me to know what she is thinking, so before planting or pruning, I'll make one clarifying request: "Just give me a vision for what you're thinking." Then with the same end in mind, we pursue it immediately and over time—we will recognize success as it blooms. In a far more wondrous way, God has a vision for what He is shaping us to be: when Christ returns, we will be like Him. We see ourselves as unworthy of this and think it to be impossible, and indeed in and of ourselves, this would be true. But God's love is transformational love, steadily pruning and growing us toward the unimaginable—to be like Jesus and to share in His glory. This is where we are going.

Then how do we become like Jesus? Must I who have been saved by faith in Christ now somehow find it within myself to change myself into His image? Thankfully, no. God's command for us is this: "to believe in the name of his Son, Jesus

Christ, and to love one another as he commanded us."[336] John tells us: "The one who keeps God's commands lives in him, and he in them. And this is how we know that he lives in us: We know it by the Spirit he gave us."[337] Long before the Messiah "became flesh and made his dwelling among us,"[338] God foretold of a day when "I will put my Spirit in you and move you to follow my decrees and be careful to keep my laws."[339] *It is through His Spirit in us that God unites us with Himself and changes us to be like Jesus in character, action, and fruitfulness.* Paul writes: "Now the Lord is the Spirit, and where the Spirit of the Lord is, there is freedom. And we all, who … contemplate the Lord's glory, are being transformed into his image with ever-increasing glory, which comes from the Lord, who is the Spirit."[340] He will never lead us in directions displeasing to God, but always in His ways of love, joy, and peace, and "against such things there is no law."[341] So today when we hear the Spirit's voice, may we open our hearts and hands to Him and follow. He will change us.

This is love: not that we loved God, but that he loved us and sent his Son as an atoning sacrifice for our sins. Dear friends, since God so loved us,

---

[336] 1 John 3:23
[337] 1 John 3:24
[338] John 1:14
[339] Ezekiel 36:27
[340] 2 Corinthians 3:17–18
[341] Galatians 5:22–23

we also ought to love one another. No one has ever seen God; but if we love one another, God lives in us and his love is made complete in us. (1 John 4:10-12)

Father, You have given us Your Spirit, who lives in us. In His power and according to Your will, make us complete in love. Transform us to be like Jesus, and be glorified in us, Your people, forever. In Christ we pray. Amen.

Afterword

R eaching this page of the book, you have read each of Paul's well-crafted reflections on various aspects of the Holy Spirit's work of transformation. Likely, you have read them one at a time as part of your daily walk with the Lord. Or maybe you could not resist reading the book straight through, cover to cover. This is the risk of reading the work of an author who is skilled in the use of the English language and equally skilled in revealing the truth of Scripture. Oh, the self-control demanded of us when reading articulate reflections wrought from God's Word! Reading Paul's short essays is a linguistic pleasure. Paul's knowledge of the Scriptures is deep. Seeing how he links together passages from various parts of the Bible is enjoyable.

Nonetheless, such experiences, though pleasant, are *not* the goal of this book. If this is all that is accomplished after reading these devotions, then we come up short. I consider the purpose of this book similar to that of a coach—a guide, an encourager in the process of transformation. An excellent coach takes the raw talent of the players and designs workouts and drills to hone their skills. The transformation starts in the preseason with rigorous training. The result of the first game of the season, win or lose, gives the coach information on how to shape successive practices in preparation for the second game, and then the third, and on and on throughout the season. Change and improvement do not cease. There is transformation for the individual athlete—greater strength, finer skills, better knowledge of the play book. There is also transformation for the team as a whole—sharper timing, precision passing, greater trust.

The same is true in the life of a Christian who encounters the transforming power of the Holy Spirit. A loss, though disappointing, is not the end of the season. There is much that can be learned from that experience. And conversely, a win, though worth celebrating, is not the end of team training. No matter whether you have experienced a failure or a success, there is always more to learn, more possibility for growth. And the need for Christian transformation resides both in the realm of individual skills—knowledge of the Scriptures, more regular prayer life, and moral excellence—and in the realm of the Body of Christ—love and forgiveness of others, service in Jesus' name, and corporate worship.

Any analogy has its limits, and there is a key aspect of Christian transformation that extends beyond a sports comparison. The transformation of a believer to be like Jesus (1 John 3:2) is not promised on the condition that we work hard enough. The Lord works His changing power in us because of who He is and because of what He has already accomplished on

162

the Cross and in the Empty Tomb. In the midst of this work of transformation, we rejoice in what He has done—past, present, and future.

I would encourage you to keep this book on a lower shelf for easy access. Reread its meditations one by one from time to time. There will be more that the Holy Spirit wants to work into (or out of) your heart. We have a patient yet persistent God who is a Master in transforming hearts and minds. We are amazed and honored that He has not given up on us, but rather will keep on working in us until our season on earth comes to its victorious conclusion.

Pastor David P. Mann, Upper Arlington Lutheran Church,
Columbus, Ohio

Acknowledgments

Thank you, Peggy Nordman and Gwen Nordman, for reviewing my manuscript through the fresh perspective of one reading it for the first time. Your insights have reached open ears, and your constructive comments have made this a better book.

Thank you, Pastor Dave Mann, for reading this book through clear theological lenses. I respect your understanding of the Word and your daily submission to its authority. God teaches and encourages me through you.

Thank you, Andrew Zager, for helping me bring this book to completion.

To the many of you who have exhorted me at points along the way to "keep writing," thank you.

About the Author

P aul Nordman authored his first book, *Christ in Me*, after retiring from executive leadership in the property-casualty insurance industry. He serves on the advisory board of The Salvation Army Columbus Area Services and is an active volunteer in Kairos Prison Ministry International, Inc. and International Friendships, Inc., a ministry to international students. Paul and his wife, Peggy, live in Columbus, Ohio, as do their son, Matthew, daughter-in-law, Gwen, and grandchildren, Abigail and Micah.

CPSIA information can be obtained
at www.ICGtesting.com
Printed in the USA
LVHW091800241120
672600LV00034B/296